THE
CHRYSALIS
CALLING

How Life's Lessons Shape Authentic Leadership

LT CARR

Table of Contents

INTRODUCTION

From pain to purpose.

The phrase may be a bit cliché. Overused. Repeated so often that its original grit has dulled from too many vision boards, Instagram captions, and motivational speeches. Even Sunday-morning preachers use it to speak of the power of using the past to shape a better present.

There is a reason it lingers. This is so much more than a catchphrase. It's a truth essential to growth—one that belongs on your screen saver, jotted in your journal, and plastered across the walls where you've placed your goals. (You do have such a wall, don't you?)

The idea of turning pain into purpose is not gentle. It is fierce, demanding, and entirely necessary. Your experiences—joyful, disorienting, heartbreaking—all serve as raw material for transformation. This may feel impossible, especially for those shaped by early loss, adversity, or trauma. And yet here we are, gathering the courage to reimagine what is possible.

To understand where we're headed, let's look at one of nature's greatest examples of real change: the butterfly. Her metamorphosis begins where many transformations begin—in stillness. Not silence, but stillness. The quiet, constricted hush of the cocoon.

Before she ever becomes a butterfly, she is something else entirely. Her story begins with an egg—a small, fragile dot clinging to the underside of a leaf. Her world is limited. She knows nothing beyond that thin surface and the faint hum of wind rocking her body back and forth. But inside that stillness, a pulse stirs. Potential. Life. A promise not yet realized.

Then she hatches—barely visible, soft-bodied, utterly unremarkable. A caterpillar. Vulnerable. Hungry. Desperate to survive. She doesn't glide. She crawls. She devours everything around her, not out of greed, but because transformation demands fuel.

She doesn't necessarily choose to change—but staying the same becomes unbearable. It's not that she hates being a caterpillar; it's that the life she's living starts to feel too small. Her skin grows tight. Her body aches with the weight of potential she can't quite name. She's grounded while something inside her longs to rise. Every day is a repeat of the last: crawl, eat, survive. No vision. No flight. No view.

Caterpillars, much like some humans, live in a state of endless hunger and slow-motion progress. And at some point, the question shifts from *"Is this safe?"* to *"Is this all there is?"* That is the turning point. Not a rejection of who she has been, but a reckoning with who she's becoming. Because no matter how familiar the ground feels, it cannot compete with the pull of waiting wings.

She doesn't change for glory—she changes because survival stops being enough. There's nothing glamorous about being a caterpillar. She lives low to the ground, exposed and vulnerable. Each leaf she chews brings nourishment and risk. She crawls because she must, dragging her own weight across rough surfaces, dodging threats she cannot outrun.

She is instinct, not insight. Consumption, not creation. And while that life may work for a time, something shifts when the body that once carried her begins to tighten like a cage. The skin that used to protect her becomes uncomfortable. She molts again and again, leaving pieces of herself behind. But even with each shedding, there is no peace. The world keeps demanding more of her—more endurance, more resilience—yet offering no shelter, no vision, no rest.

Eventually, weariness outpaces hunger. And somewhere deep inside, without fully understanding why, she knows: staying like this will kill her just as surely as transformation might. Remaining a caterpillar means living in constant reaction—never safe, never seen, never imagining what it means to soar.

That is why you are here reading these words. You know you are a leader—or meant to become a better one. You feel the pull toward something higher. But you can't quite figure out how to get there. My hope is that by the time you turn the last page, your process of metamorphosis will be well underway.

Let me warn you—the decision to outgrow comfort isn't easy. Self-reflection is grueling. It wasn't painless for me, and it won't be painless for you.

There were years when I was all hunger. Years when I clawed at life, trying to make sense of who I was, what I was worth, and why my story felt more like a cautionary tale than a calling. Years when other people's dysfunction spilled into my life, leaving stains I feared I would never cleanse.

My identity was built on proving myself to people who never planned to see me. Titles, clout, and the illusion of security felt like salves for open wounds. I hustled because I was terrified—not of failure, but of being seen *in* my failure. My shell cracked. My skin split. Still, I kept going.

Then came the stillness. The darkness. The chrysalis.

We romanticize the cocoon, don't we? Imagine it as a sacred pause, a gentle unfolding, like some spa retreat for caterpillars. But science tells another story. Most of her former self dissolves. She becomes a soupy mess. Her old form dies—completely. Unrecognizable. Vulnerable in the extreme. Only then, from the mess, do specific cells that have existed in her all along begin to activate. They don't fight for attention. They collaborate. They build something new from what was broken.

That's where I found myself: in the soup. Everything I once used to define myself was stripped away. I didn't recognize the reflection staring back at me. But inside that breakdown, something stirred __not all at once, not in a blaze of clarity, but gradually. Quietly.

It started with acceptance. That happens to be the first stage of my framework, grounded in AGT · Acceptance. Growth. Transformation.

Let me pause here and return to the caterpillar. When her body dissolves, where does it go? The answer: she eats it. Every drop. I'm going to encourage you to do the same.

This book is an invitation to see transformation through a new lens. I hope to convince you that you can use *everything* you once were to fuel who you want to be.

Leadership isn't about becoming someone else. It's about becoming more of the best of who you already are—beneath the fear, the doubt, the layers of armor you've been told to wear. It's about using the obstacles, not avoiding them. It's about recognizing that adversity is a crucible, not a curse.

Let me say it again: adversity is a crucible, not a curse.

I used to think my past disqualified me from leadership __that my story was too messy. That I needed to clean it up, tuck it in, and serve it cold to be taken seriously. But the more I coached, listened, and lived, the more I realized how backward that thinking was. The mess *is* the message. My pain isn't a side note—it's the soil. And like that caterpillar who has no idea she is destined for flight, I had to sit in the dark long enough to let those creative cells do their work.

This book is not for the faint of heart. It's for leaders who are tired of pretending. For those who look successful on paper but feel hollow in their chests. For high-achievers who check the boxes and still can't sleep. For those building companies, teams, and families—but losing themselves in the process.

It's for the ones who've been through hell but still want to lead with empathy and strength, who make room for others but have no room left for themselves.

Yes. They will.

This book will show you how—not by giving easy answers, but by helping you ask better questions. Not by granting permission (you already have that), but by offering perspective. And if I do my job well, by giving you hope and processes to unearth the best you have available.

The most powerful leaders are not the ones with all the answers—they are the ones who have done their inner work. Those who have metabolized their pain into purpose. Who sit with discomfort without rushing to fix it. Who tell the truth—even when their voice shakes.

Those are the leaders I coach. Those are the leaders I write for. Those are the leaders the world desperately needs.

In these pages, you'll find parts of my story: the daughter who learned to stay small to keep the peace, the professional who learned to take up space with grace. The young woman who mistook perfectionism for excellence. The grown woman who learned to forgive herself, over and over again. You'll meet the caterpillar, the cocoon, and the butterfly—sometimes all in the same chapter.

You'll also meet the Butterfly Affect model, a framework I've developed through years of guiding leaders through transformative growth. It's rooted in my lived journey as a nurse, leader, and leader of leaders—shaped by the transformations I've witnessed in others. It's a window where your hard-earned wisdom can find expression. A survival guide for leaders who didn't take the fast track but the one littered with sharp turns, cracked pavement, and the occasional miracle.

And no, "Affect" is not a typo. This framework is about how you *affect* those you lead—and the impact you have on their growth.

I've sat across from CEOs, founders, creatives, educators, and changemakers from every walk of life. And despite their differences, they all shared one truth: they were becoming. Unfolding. Shedding. Molting. Rebuilding—again and again.

Authentic leadership is not static. Not a title. Not tenure. It's a posture of becoming. So if you're in a season of breakdown, I see you. If you're questioning everything—your path, your purpose, your power—I get it. If you've outgrown the skin you're in and you're terrified of what's next but can't go back, I'm walking with you.

Together, we'll explore how to Accept what is. Grow from what was. And Transform into what could be.

Let's go. Your butterfly awaits.

"You couldn't relive your life, skipping the awful parts, without losing what made it worthwhile. You have to accept it as a whole--like the world itself."

— Stewart O'Nan, The Odds: A Love Story

CHAPTER 1 – NO NAME, NO PLACE

I know all about unhappy beginnings.

I was born the youngest of eleven children—three from my mother and eight from my father's previous relationships. One would think that with so many siblings I would have been immersed in the connection that comes with a large family. I never felt that way. The sense of belonging that should have embraced me always seemed just out of reach.

My father was a man I never met, a man who died before I could hear his voice, feel his touch, or experience his fierce protection from the wolves lying in wait to steal everything of value about me.

I entered the world already halfway written out of it. He passed away 51 days before I was born—young, sick, and gone without warning. Poor health, they said. But what does a baby know about poor health or sudden death or the way absence can echo louder than presence? All I knew was a gap, a hole, an ache that would never heal on this side of heaven.

All I had were pictures. Stills of a man with dark eyes and a quiet strength I tried to imagine into motion. My mother showed them to me at times, but she never lingered. She—loved him that much I knew. But by the time I came along, they weren't legally married.

No Hyphen to connect us. No legal bond. No proof. Just a belly full of me and a man already slipping into memory.

I didn't even get his name.

Not on my birth certificate. Not in lineage conversations. Not in the whispers of legacy floating around my older siblings who had the privilege of claiming him. My sister got his name. But me? I was the asterisk. The exception. The question mark. I entered the world not just fatherless, but nameless. And let me tell you—children notice that. Even when no one speaks it aloud, even when adults try to sugarcoat the silence, we feel it in our bones.

It haunts you. It sits on your shoulder like a shadow that never quite touches the ground.

My mother was a single parent raising three children—my sister, my brother, and me. I was her last. Maybe her mistake. Maybe her redemption. It depended on the day. She was strong, but not soft. She did what she had to do, and tenderness wasn't always on the list.

She remarried a man older, harder, and full of rage. Liquor-induced rage that made him cold and distant or fiery and abusive. If he was mad, he let her know. But my mother was no shrinking violet. She stood her ground. She didn't go quietly or gently. She pushed back with the fury of someone who had already lost too much and refused to lose any more.

I was just a toddler, sitting in corners, hiding behind furniture, watching it all unfold.

Chaos like that seeps into your nervous system before you even learn the words for it. I learned to read rooms before I learned to read books. I could tell by the pitch of a footstep whether the night would end in silence or screams. Survival is a language, and I became fluent early.

When my mother worked—which was often—she left us with people she trusted. One of them violated that trust. This person watched us most days.

I was four years old the day this individual sexually assaulted me.

Four.

They waited until the house was quiet and slid a knife into the crack of the bedroom door, jamming it shut so no one could come in. They knew my brother was due home soon. They didn't care. They counted on fear. Silence. Obedience. They counted on me staying small.

I don't remember pain. I tried to search my body for that detail—for years I tried. It never comes. But I remember knowing. The thick, sick feeling that something was terribly wrong. That what was happening wasn't love, wasn't play, wasn't anything meant to be held inside my tiny body. But he warned me. He told me not to speak. And at four years old, I learned the weight of a secret I didn't ask to carry.

That moment shaped me—not just the act, but the silence afterward.

I learned that my safety was negotiable. That my body was not mine. That trusted people could turn cruel. I learned how to disappear in plain sight, how to nod when I wanted to scream, how to smile while my stomach twisted into knots. I learned unworthiness like it was a second language. And once you learn it, it's hard to unlearn.

There were more lessons—less dramatic but just as sharp.

I remember struggling to learn how to tie my shoes before preschool—still at the age of four. My mother operated in survival mode most days, carrying burdens that left little room for gentleness. She understood the world as harsh and unforgiving and believed I needed to be prepared to face it.

When I couldn't tie my shoes, she disciplined me. She spanked me and sent me to the corner, insisting I stay there until I figured it out. Whether it was time or tenderness she lacked, I can only guess—but what I remember is the silence, the pressure, and the lesson that struggle was mine to manage. I stared at those tangled laces like they held the secret to something more than shoes. As if cracking the code might unlock something softer.

Eventually, I did. I taught myself how to tie my shoes.

Shortly after, I was enrolled in preschool. I had one friend—AP. Shy. Soft-spoken. One day his mother found me crouched beside him, teaching him how to tie his shoes. She chuckled. "Look at her helping you out." I smiled, but I wasn't doing it for praise.

In my young mind, the penalty for not knowing how to tie shoes was a spanking. I didn't want AP to experience what I had.

That's how early the wiring gets set. I wasn't just being a good friend. I was trying to protect someone from the shame I knew too well. Once you've been hit for being slow, you never look at another person's struggle the same way. You start seeing behind behavior. You start hearing what isn't said.

You learn to lead with empathy before anyone calls it a skill.

That was the beginning of the fracture—and the foundation.

On one side: the trauma. The namelessness. The chaos. The betrayal. The bruises that faded and the ones that didn't.

On the other: the noticing. The helping. The instinct to protect. The early flame of something strong and sacred inside me that refused to be snuffed out.

I didn't know it then, but those two sides—pain and purpose—would chase each other for years. They would dance, collide, compete, and eventually converge.

And that's where my story begins.

Not with a last name. Not with a father's legacy. But with a girl in the corner, staring at her shoes, trying to figure out how to make something hold.

I turned my pain and experiences toward helping someone else.

REFLECTION EXERCISES

"What parts of my past or present have I been avoiding because they feel too painful or messy to face? Why?"

"In what situations do I find myself pretending to be okay when I'm not? What would it feel like to tell the truth instead?"

"What truths about myself am I afraid to admit—even to me? Take a deep breath and write them. Then take another and speak them aloud."

"What would it mean for me to fully accept where I am right now without labeling it as failure or success—just reality?"

CHAPTER 2 – LEARN THE ART OF ACCEPTANCE

My past could read like a crime scene. Broken glass, bloodstains, no witnesses willing to testify, and a knife in the door. I don't say that for shock value—I say it because it's true. And because too many of us are still dragging the past behind us like dead weight, pretending it's not heavy.

For years, I was one of those people—walking around carrying invisible burdens, not realizing how much of the past still had its grip on me. I wore it like a second skin. You couldn't always see it, but it shaped everything: the tone of my voice in meetings, the way I flinched at criticism, the way I distrusted praise, the way I took on too much to prove I was enough. My history didn't just live in my memory; it bled into how I led, how I listened, how I reacted. Every decision I made, every interaction I had, carried the silent echo of what I had survived. I thought if I moved fast enough—achieved more, worked harder, stayed busier, I could outrun the shadows. But the truth is, unexamined pain doesn't disappear. It just finds new ways to speak.

People who've had a complicated past often lead from a place of self-protection rather than purpose. We confuse control with clarity. We mistake urgency for excellence. And instead of creating safety for others, we build walls that keep everyone—including ourselves—at a distance.

I was wrong.

Let me tell you what it really looked like.

When my father died, my mother didn't grieve out loud. She hardened. Her sadness turned inward and calcified into resentment. She'd say things like, "He left me with these kids," as if we were groceries dumped on a doorstep, not human beings. As if we weren't just as abandoned as she was. I was too young to understand mental illness. A distant mother doesn't just withhold affection—she alters the blueprint of how her children learn to give and receive love. Not on purpose. Not maliciously. Often, she's doing the best she can with what she has. But absence, emotional or physical, still leaves a mark.

Children of emotionally unavailable mothers often become adults who confuse love with earning. We learn to anticipate needs before they're spoken, to stay small and agreeable so we don't provoke withdrawal. We mistake caretaking for connection. We overextend ourselves trying to feel wanted, not realizing that we're replicating the emotional imbalance in which we were raised.

I was one of those children. I learned that love was conditional—given when I was useful, withheld when I needed too much. I didn't learn how to sit still in affection, to be loved without performing, to feel safe when I wasn't being productive. As a result, I entered into relationships—both personal and professional—with a distorted sense of worth. I tolerated too much. I over functioned. I mistook peace for silence and closeness for control.

"But mostly, you learned to fend for yourself," says my therapist.

And I did.

I learned to cook real meals—no peanut butter and jelly here. I'm talking rice and beans, stews, fried chicken when it was available, and whatever stretched the farthest when it wasn't. I stood on a chair in the kitchen, stirring pots and making sure there was something to eat. I stepped up—not because I had to, but because it was needed. I was still a child, yet in those moments, the house required a grown-up. So I became one. These were the early signs of my adaptability, care for others, and, yes, leadership. Leaders step up and fill the void. I learned this in the most tender years of my childhood.

My mother had a few relationships over the years—none of them lasting long, and most of them marked by pain. Only one ever seemed serious, stable, promising even. But that too ended in heartbreak when he disappeared without warning, leaving behind no explanation—only silence and shattered hope. After that, something in her hardened for good. She swore off men entirely. But by then, the damage had already been done—not just to her heart, but to our lives.

Before she gave up on relationships, we were dragged through a revolving door of instability. We moved often. My mother always managed to find a place—sometimes small, often temporary—but always ours. Every place felt temporary. We packed and unpacked our lives too frequently, drifting through spaces like ghosts, never truly settled or safe.

What made it harder was that we rarely lived alone. There was almost always someone else staying with us—cousins, family friends, people who needed a place just like we did. At the time, it felt unfair. What little we had, or didn't have, was constantly being stretched even thinner. I used to believe that if we could just keep what was ours, maybe it would finally be enough for us—for me. It took years to understand the quiet power in family pooling their "little" together to make it work. Back then, though, it just felt like giving away the very thing we were still desperate to find—security.

By my junior year of high school, my mother and I were homeless. I remember stuffing my clothes into a black trash bag—because there was no suitcase, no closet, no dresser to claim as mine. That bag held everything I owned, and I carried it as if it were an extension of me. I went to church for two reasons: to hear words of hope, encouragement, and healing—and to find someone kind enough to let me spend the night so I could make it to school the next day. Free lunch was a lifesaver back then.

Eventually, we got accepted into a housing project. And as strange as it sounds, that was a blessing. It wasn't glamorous; it was survival.

But none of that healed me. It just gave me a place to hide the damage.

For a long time, I lived inside my story like it was the only one that mattered. I wallowed. I bathed in the injustice of it all. I felt righteous in my rage. And don't get me wrong—your anger is valid. It's earned. But you can't build a future out of fury. At some point, I had to stop asking, "Why did this happen to me?" and start asking, "What am I going to do with it?"

That's when I discovered the quiet power of the art of acceptance.

And let me be clear: acceptance is not surrender. It's not approval. It's not a soft kind of forgiveness that makes everyone else comfortable. No. Acceptance is truth-telling. It's standing in front of the mirror and saying, "It left its mark, but it doesn't get to hold the pen."

Yes, the past can shape how we walk, but it doesn't get to say where we're going.

Acceptance is opening the door to your past and walking through it—not locking it up and pretending it never happened, and not frantically looking for some other door to escape through.

There is only one door that leads to healing for effective leaders: the door of acceptance. Looking squarely at your history and simply nodding.

We think the past is either a predictor or a prison. We use it as an anchor or a prophecy. We say things like, "I can't lead because no one will follow me." "I can't succeed because I was born behind." "I can't trust people because I've been betrayed." And all of those statements may carry hints of truth. But the fuller truth is this: your past is a resource. A library. A toolbox. If you're brave enough to sift through the wreckage, you'll find exactly what you need to lead with integrity.

The key is learning how to leverage your experience instead of being ruled by it.

Most humans focus on the problem rather than the root cause. And most root causes live in us. In our wiring. In our wounds.

You're not truly leading until you understand why raised voices make you shrink, why success feels unsafe, or why you hesitate unless everyone approves. That's not leadership—that's reaction. That's managing your triggers, not your team. I say this with compassion, because I've lived it.

As a young leader, I wanted to make a good impression. I wanted to give answers. I thought leadership meant being the strongest voice in the room. But real leadership starts with telling yourself the truth. The whole truth. Even the ugly parts.

I remember a story from the Bible—whether you're religious or not, it holds a lesson. There was a man named Nathan. He was a prophet during the reign of King David. David had power. Status. Legacy. He also had secrets. He had done something shameful and used that power to conceal it. God sent Nathan—not to flatter, but to confront.

Nathan didn't walk in with a sword. He walked in with a story. He told David about a rich man who stole a poor man's only lamb. David, indignant, said the rich man should be punished. Nathan looked him in the eye and said, "You are that man."

That moment still gives me chills. Because that's what leadership needs: people willing to speak truth to power—and power that's willing to listen.

Eventually, you will meet your flaws like a train in the face. You can either brace for impact or build the track.

I had to learn to surround myself with people who weren't afraid of my title. People who would tell me when I was slipping. People who'd say, "You're leading from your wound right now, not your wisdom." That kind of feedback stings—but it saves you. It saved me.

So what does this mean for you?

It means start small. It's not about dramatic transformations. You don't need to reinvent yourself in a week. You just need to make one honest change. Ask one hard question. Let one person in. Accept one truth about your past—not to wallow in it, but to understand it. To extract the lesson instead of re-living the pain.

Because leadership isn't about perfection. It's about presence.

It's about showing up with your full self—scars and all—and saying, *"This is where I've been. This is what I've learned. And this is how I lead because of it."*

REFLECTION EXERCISES

Purpose: Heal and repurpose painful memories.

We all carry reminders of where we've been—some obvious, some tucked away. A black trash bag from nights of homelessness. A school report card that whispered, "not enough." A kitchen tool you used to feed a family because no one else would.

These objects hold energy. They remind us of survival, yes—but also of pain.

But what if you could change the story they tell?

Here's your invitation:

At your own pace, consider a physical object that reminds you of a hard season. It does not need to carry the full story, just something like a hospital bracelet, a notebook, a pair of shoes, a set of keys, or another object connected to an experience you moved through. Now, transform it.

- Decorate it.

- Paint it.

- Cover it in affirmations.

- Turn it into art.

- Make it useful in a new way.

For example:

- Turn a black trash bag into a reusable tote covered in words that remind you of your strength.

- Frame a scrap of fabric that once represented struggle and display it as a symbol of how far you've come.

- Sand and paint an old chair to sit taller and prouder in your new life.

This is more than arts and crafts. It's alchemy. You're taking something that once felt heavy and turning it into something powerful. You're proving to yourself that you're not just a product of what happened to you. You're the artist, the creator, the author of what comes next.

When you look at your reclaimed object, you'll remember: **You're not defined by your past. You're the one who gets to redefine it.**

Now that you're done, spend a few minutes writing about how you feel about that life incident:

CHAPTER 3 – EXPOSE, HELP, LEAD

They say time heals all wounds.

It doesn't.

Time teaches you how to live with the wound. How to dress it so it doesn't scare people. How to tuck it under a sleeve or behind a smile. But healing—real healing—requires more than time. It requires purpose. And for me, that purpose began to rise when I started reaching back. Helping others. Pulling people out of the same darkness I once thought would drown me.

That's where healing starts—not in isolation, but in connection.

Many people believe Harriet Tubman was the Underground Railroad's only conductor. But the truth is, there were many. Free Black men and women, abolitionists, stationmasters, pastors, farmers—people who had already tasted liberation but couldn't stomach enjoying it alone. They had seen slavery up close. Heard the screams. Felt the whips. Smelled the sweat and blood in the air. Some had escaped it. Others had been born free. But none were untouched. None were fully free. Because you can leave the plantation and still be haunted by the memory.

And that's what compelled them to return.

Imagine that for a moment. You've clawed your way to freedom. You have a chance to finally rest, to start over. But the ghosts of those you left behind won't let you sleep. And instead of silencing that ache, you let it move you. You pick up a lantern, memorize the paths through the woods, and you risk your life—not for your own freedom, but for someone else's.

That is legacy.
That is leadership.

Many believe that once you heal, grow, or "make it," the journey is over. But real transformation doesn't end with your breakthrough—it invites you to reach back.

There are leaders, mentors, guides—not by title, but by choice. People who have walked through their own fires of loss, rejection, burnout, or trauma. And instead of using their freedom to escape, they use it to build a bridge.

Imagine climbing out of a deep pit—nails bloodied, heart aching— and once you reach the top, instead of running toward safety, you turn around. You anchor a rope. You shine a light. Not because it's easy, but because you know someone else is still down there... and you remember exactly how that darkness felt.

That's what leadership born from pain looks like. Not performative. Not positional. But purposeful. It's not about proving your strength. It's about refusing to hoard your healing. You can't be a positive leader if your fists are clenched.

There's an old parable about an ingenious way an African tribe caught monkeys. They built a simple wooden box with a small hole in the side, just big enough for a monkey to slide its hand through. Inside was a banana or some other treat. The monkey, curious, would reach in and grab the prize. But with its hand now clenched around the fruit, it couldn't pull it back out. It was trapped. Not because of the box, but because it refused to let go. The monkey could have been free. It *was* free. But it chose to stay bound.

We are not so different.

We hold onto our pain like it's proof. Proof that we were wronged. Evidence that we deserve pity. Proof that we're justified in our fear, our anger, our distance. And maybe we are. But we can't be free while holding tight to the very thing that's keeping us stuck.

Pain has a shelf life. Let it teach you what it needs to teach you—and then let it go. Otherwise, the rot, mold, and decay spread to other parts of your being.

That open hand?
That's where the healing starts.
That's where the helping begins.

I remember standing in line at the local bakery as a little girl, watching other children point at pastries and pick out donuts with sprinkles while their parents handed over cash and smiled. I stood there with my face pressed to the glass, looking at sweetness I couldn't touch. No one asked if I wanted something. No one looked twice. And I learned something hard that day—that people can know you're in need and still not help.

They're too busy. Too uncomfortable. Too unsure if they have enough for themselves.

But I also remember whispering to myself, "If I ever have the chance, I'll be the one who shares."

That became a vow.

Because the truth is, it costs nothing to pay attention. To notice. To offer a little kindness to someone running on fumes. You don't need a title to lead. You don't need a budget to bless. You just need to unclench your hand.

I often ask myself:
What did I need when I was in need?

And whatever the answer is, I try to become it for someone else.

That is leadership.

It's not about making a name for yourself. It's not about gaining followers or stacking accolades. It's about being the change agent. The interrupter. The one who sees the wound and doesn't turn away. The one who, like Harriet, like Nathan, like the woman with the oil in the Bible, chooses to show up anyway.

There's a story in Scripture about a widow who had nothing left but a small jar of oil. The prophet Elijah tells her to pour. She doubts. She's scared. But she trusts. And as she pours the oil into empty jars, the miracle happens: the oil never runs out.

It only stops flowing when she runs out of vessels.

In other words—
as long as you keep pouring, you'll be filled.

This is the principle of reciprocity. The more you give, the more you receive. Not always in material form, but in energy. In purpose. In clarity. If your soul is feeling dry, if your work feels empty, if your relationships feel strained—check your pour. You may be holding back. You may be clenching your fists. But remember: closed fists can't receive. If you want to be poured into, you must be willing to pour out.

It's the same lesson from the boy with the five loaves and two fish. He didn't have much. But what he had, he offered. And in the hands of God, it multiplied. Fed thousands.

That's how legacy works.

I am not a reservoir. I don't hoard what I've been given. I'm a conduit. A channel. A vessel. What flows to me, flows through me. And the more I release, the more I'm refilled.

There's a Lenten prayer I return to often—
It's not about me.
It's simple. Humbling. It recalibrates my heart. Because ego is loud. Ego wants to protect, control, and perform. But service is quiet and strong. It listens. It lifts. It loves.

As a leader, especially one who has come through adversity, the temptation is to build walls—to protect yourself from being used, disappointed, or let down again. But leadership isn't about insulation. It's about incarnation.
Less of me.
More of Thee.
Less protecting.
More participating.

"If I can help somebody as I walk along, then my living will not be in vain."

Helping others is the knife out of the door.

You remember that story—the knife jammed into the bedroom door to trap me in silence and pain. That memory used to keep me up at night. But now I see it differently. That knife isn't just part of my trauma. It's part of my triumph. Because every time I open my hand, every time I tell my story, every time I show up for someone else— that blade loosens. The door opens. And I become the woman I needed back then.

That is freedom.
That is power.
That is leadership.

REFLECTION EXERCISES

In this chapter, we asked a very important question:

"What did I need when I was in need?"

This question isn't just about looking back. It's a bridge between your past and the kind of leader—and human—you want to be now.

Here's your invitation:

Find a quiet place. Sit comfortably. Close your eyes. Take three slow breaths in and out. Let your shoulders drop. Let your jaw unclench.

When you feel ready, ask yourself gently:

"What did I need when I was in my hardest moments?"

Don't rush the answer. Let memories rise. You might think of childhood. Or a heartbreak. Or a time at work when you felt alone.

Did you need someone to listen without fixing? Did you need kindness? Safety? Encouragement? A soft place to land?

When you feel the answer, open your eyes and write it down.

Then ask yourself:

"How can I offer this same thing to the people I lead, to my family, or even to strangers?"

Because leadership isn't just about driving results, it's about becoming the person you once needed.

Carry this meditation into your week. Notice moments when you can become someone else's answer to the question you've just asked.

And remember—sometimes the healing you give away is the healing you keep.

CHAPTER 4: THE POWER OF THE PEN

So, everything I've said so far sounds good in theory. Growth. Healing. Helping others. Open hands. All of it is beautiful and true.

But let's be honest: how do you actually find the strength to face your past? To wade through the fog of old wounds, betrayal, trauma, and confusion without getting stuck there?

How do you grow without crumbling?

You start by picking up a pen. That's it.

Not a program. Not a therapy session. Not a retreat in the mountains or a 90-day cleanse. Just a pen. Of course, I am all for programs and therapies. And we all need a good mountain retreat from time to time. But the daily work is inner work. It is done partly on our knees (which I will cover later and which is not just for religious people) and with our hand.

You write.

Before you roll your eyes or tune out, I want you to hear me: most people have journaling all wrong. That's why they say it doesn't work. And that's why they don't reap its benefits.

Journaling isn't about writing perfect paragraphs. It's not an essay. It's not even a full sentence if you don't want it to be. Journaling is a release. A witness. A quiet little revolution between you and the page.

And no, you don't have to do it every day. And no, you don't have to be good at it. You just have to start.

A lot of people are intimidated by journaling because they think it has to look a certain way. Or maybe they've tried it before and failed. They sat down with a beautiful notebook, wrote for two days, then forgot it under a pile of laundry. Been there. But journaling isn't about consistency—it's about connection. Connection to yourself, your thoughts, your patterns, your emotions, your future.

You can start with a sticky note.

You can start with a doodle. A feeling. A single word.

Sometimes mine just says "pause."

That's it. One word that reminds me to stop spinning, stop rushing, stop reacting. Pausing is power. It's not weakness. It's wisdom.

Our ancestors knew this. Journaling isn't new-age fluff. It's ancestral intelligence. Harriet Tubman couldn't risk keeping a journal, but many who walked beside her did—documenting maps, stories, signs, and thoughts. James Baldwin wrote his pain and truth into journals long before it became published prose. Marcus Aurelius, one of the most powerful Roman emperors, filled page after page with reflections that now make up *Meditations*. Leonardo da Vinci wrote observations, inventions, and confessions into his journals. Frida Kahlo, Anne Frank, Malcolm X, and so many others have poured their lives onto pages—raw, messy, brilliant pages.

Journaling is legacy-building in real time.

It is the bridge between growth and transformation. It is the space where the "what happened to me" becomes "what I understand about me."

Try this: pull out a memory that won't leave you alone. One that tugs at the edge of your mind. Maybe it was something someone said that stuck in your skin. Maybe it was the first time you felt shame. Or joy. Or rage. Write about it. Not with judgment—just curiosity.

What were you feeling?
Where were you standing?
What did your body do?

Then—immediately after writing—do something that makes you feel good. Something small but nourishing. A favorite song. A warm drink. A slow breath. Reinforce the act of reflection with reward. That's how you create safety around your healing process. A popular radio psychiatrist used to say, "Never walk into the dark without first lighting a candle." So light yours.

Your journal is your candle.

You can also journal your emotions. Ask yourself: *When was the first time I felt this way?* That question will take you places. It brings the past into focus not to haunt you, but to help you understand where your reactions come from. It's not about wallowing. It's about witnessing.

Once you understand yourself, you begin to self-regulate.

Leadership is about that pause—before the email, before the clapback, before the shutdown. It's choosing presence over performance. It's interacting from a place of understanding, not emotion. And one of the fastest ways to practice this is through physical mindfulness. Try this:

- Inhale through your nose for 3 counts

- Hold for 4

- Exhale slowly through your mouth for 7

- Relax your pelvic floor while you do it (yes, seriously—clenching there is a stress signal)

You can write that breathing pattern down in your journal. Use it during high-stress meetings, or after a conflict, or before a tough decision. That's the real work of leadership—not reacting.

Now let's talk about goal setting. This is the part where transformation starts to bloom.

Write your goals down.

Be specific. Give them deadlines.

Not vague hopes like, "I want to go back to school." No. Write: "I will be a registered nurse by June 1, 2027."

That clarity gives your brain a direction. It takes your dreams seriously. Even if your circumstances don't line up yet, your intention sets something in motion. (You may want to create a visual "Goal Sheet"—I'll show you how later.)

But don't stop there.

Negative circumstances must be faced and quickly forgiven. Yes, forgive your bad days, too.

Write about them in the same journal. This is not to relive the failure, but to learn from it. Start with what went wrong—but don't stay there. Ask yourself: *"If I was at my best, I would have…"* That question rewires your brain. It turns guilt into growth. It helps you coach yourself. The next time you face that situation, this journal entry is likely to pop into your head.

Then finish the entry with this: *"One thing I did well today was…"* and mean it. Train yourself to see the good—even if the only thing you did well was get out of bed. That still counts.

Because reflection without kindness becomes cruelty. You must take expert care of yourself and allow no one to dump on you. Even you. Your journal isn't a courtroom. It's a companion. It doesn't exist to punish or shame you. It's a space to meet yourself with truth and compassion. It's where you begin to close the loop on the parts of yourself that have been left hanging—unheard, unseen, unspoken.

Your journal will reveal patterns in you. You'll start to see what drains you, what triggers you, what lifts you up. You'll track growth without needing a spreadsheet. You'll notice when your boundaries start slipping. You'll hear yourself more clearly.

And in time, your journal becomes a map. A map back to who you are. A map forward to who you're becoming.

So, whether you write in a leather-bound journal, a grocery store notebook, or scribble on the back of receipts, just start. Write the mess. Write the miracle. Write the real. Then you are empowered to write the future.

Because the greatest leader you will ever follow is the one you are becoming.

REFLECTION EXERCISES

GOAL SETTING

DATE:

VISION

MISSION

STRATEGY

ACTION PLANS

CHAPTER 5: RADICAL SELF-HONESTY

Radical self-honesty is not for the faint of heart. It is not about beating yourself up. It's not self-criticism dressed up in fancier language. No—radical self-honesty is about looking in the mirror and deciding that, this time, you're not going to blink. You're going to tell the truth, the *whole* truth, even the parts that make you squirm. Especially those parts.

It's easy to become fluent in other people's flaws. I could write a dissertation on what went wrong in my marriage if I focused only on him—his moods, his emotional unavailability, his stubbornness, the way he tuned me out when I needed him to lean in. That list? I've rehearsed it more than once.

But the truth—the radical truth—is that I had a part in that unraveling too.
I wasn't always encouraging.
I didn't build my husband up.
I expected him to be more while I gave less.
I withheld affection when I didn't feel heard.
I thought I was punishing him, but in the end, I was starving the relationship.

I own it. Every painful inch of it. Not to shame myself, but to grow. To do better next time. To become the kind of person who can lead in life and love with integrity.

Owning your part doesn't mean excusing the other person. It means you stop letting their behavior be the only story you tell.
It means reclaiming your power by taking responsibility for the way you showed up—or didn't.

This applies just as much in leadership as it does in love.

When I moved from charge nurse to supervisor, I thought I was ready. I knew the policies. I knew the protocols. I knew the people. I thought those things made me qualified to lead. What I didn't realize is that leadership is less about what you know and more about how you make others feel.

My promotion moved me from buddy to boss, and I didn't know how to handle the shift. I thought leadership meant command. Direction. Correction. So that's what I did. I told people what to do. I corrected their errors. I pointed out inefficiencies. I expected compliance.

And I failed.

My team started calling me "Super Nurse"—not as a compliment, but as a dig. It stung. But looking back, I understand why. I had forgotten to lead with humanity. I had stepped into the role without building relationships. I hadn't earned trust. I hadn't created psychological safety. I wanted performance without partnership—authority without alignment. I tried to lead with power instead of presence.

Radical self-honesty forced me to step back—not just emotionally, but practically.
I started analyzing my behavior like a coach reviewing game tape.

What did I do well?
Where did I overreach?
What assumptions was I making?
How were my words landing?
What did I miss?

I began to see a pattern. I was using my versatility—my ability to jump into any role, take on any task, solve any problem—as a shield. I thought being the most capable person in the room was the point. But all it did was isolate me. I didn't realize how much I needed others to succeed.

Talent and character are not the same thing.
Your talent can get you promoted.
Your character determines whether you can sustain it.

My talent made me fast, effective, and respected. But it also made me impatient. I struggled to watch people learn at their own pace. I didn't give people room to try, fail, and grow. And if you're not giving your people that space, you're not leading—you're managing. Maybe even micromanaging.

The smartest thing I did?
I stopped showing off how smart I was.

I started asking more questions.
I invited opinions.
I created room for ideas that weren't mine.

And something incredible happened—my team started to come alive.
They started to trust me.
They started to lead.

I learned to make space.
Not just space for myself, but space for others to shine.

I began to see leadership not as the act of standing in front, but as the art of stepping aside. I stopped needing to be the smartest voice in the room and started being the person who made it safe for other smart voices to speak up. I invited people to bring their gifts to the table, their ideas, their creativity, their lived experiences—and I listened. Truly listened.

When people feel seen, they step into their brilliance.
When people feel heard, they begin to lead themselves.

That's the environment I wanted to create. One where my team didn't feel they had to prove themselves to me, but instead felt empowered to be themselves around me.

Making space is not just metaphorical—it's practical.
It means not jumping in to solve problems right away.
It means asking, "What do *you* think?" and really meaning it.
It means noticing who hasn't spoken in a meeting and creating an opening for their voice.
It means praising ideas that aren't your own and allowing your team's creativity to eclipse your ego.

This is what strong leaders do: they cultivate environments where others can display their talents, stretch their capacity, and experience what it feels like to be believed in.

That's where collaboration begins.

The word *collaboration* comes from the Latin *collaborare*, which means "to work together." True collaboration isn't about splitting tasks or simply being on the same team. It's about co-creating. Mutual respect. Shared responsibility. The kind of trust that allows for disagreement without destruction. It's understanding that no one person has a monopoly on wisdom.

When we work together—when we *truly* collaborate—we're stronger, wiser, and more innovative than we could ever be alone.

Collaboration requires humility.
It means checking your need to be right at the door.
It means believing someone else's insight might take the idea further than you ever could alone.
It's not about being the hero—it's about building something bigger than any one person's contribution.

Collaboration is not a buzzword. It's a leadership necessity. It means letting go of the need to control every outcome and instead trusting the process—and the people. It means creating a culture where people feel safe to contribute, challenge, and create. It means celebrating not just what gets done, but *how* it gets done—through connection, dialogue, and shared purpose.

Radical self-honesty isn't easy. It forces you to examine the parts of yourself that are still in progress. It holds a mirror up to your blind spots. But it also gives you the one thing no title ever will: clarity.

And with clarity comes growth.

So I ask you, as a leader, a partner, a person navigating your life:

Where are you telling half-truths to yourself?
Where are you letting your talent hide your character flaws?
Where are you avoiding responsibility by focusing on what they did instead of what you allowed?

Because until you get honest, you'll stay stuck.

But the moment you do—that's where everything begins to change. That's where transformation begins.

But let's talk about how transformation is often disguised—how it rarely comes wrapped in clarity and courage and more often shows up looking like crisis. Breakdown can look like failure. It can feel like shame, panic, confusion, or loss. But if you're willing to be radically honest, that same breakdown can become the very doorway into your breakthrough.

When things fall apart—when you're sitting in the wreckage of your best efforts—that's when truth has the most room to speak. But only if you're willing to listen.

Most people rush to escape discomfort, patch things up quickly, pretend it wasn't that bad. But radical self-honesty says: *pause.* Don't reach for the quick fix. Sit with what broke. Ask why it broke. Ask what part you played. And then, instead of blaming or deflecting, you start gathering wisdom from the ruins.

Every breakthrough I've experienced—personal, professional, spiritual—was preceded by a moment of breakdown that forced me to look inward. Not to punish myself, but to re-center. To recalibrate. That is the gift of radical honesty: it allows you to mine your lowest moments for the lessons that will elevate your life.

So the next time something falls apart, ask yourself:
Is this a breakdown—or the beginning of a breakthrough?

The difference is your willingness to tell the truth… about *yourself.*

This requires an attribute often in short supply in our world: humility.

REFLECTION EXERCISES

Speak A Hard Truth

Out loud, speak **one radical truth about yourself** that you've been avoiding.

Examples:

- *"I use my busyness to avoid feeling lonely."*

- *"I get defensive when someone points out my mistakes."*

- *"I want people to think I'm perfect because I'm afraid they'll leave if they see my flaws."*

- *"I lead from fear when I feel insecure."*

It doesn't have to be eloquent. It must be honest.

Pause. Notice how it feels to hear it spoken. Don't look away.

CHAPTER 6: HUMILITY IN LEADERSHIP – REAL STORIES, LASTING IMPACT

Coming out of radical self-honesty, there's a natural next step:
humility.
If self-honesty reveals what's true about us, humility reveals what's
possible through us.

In a world obsessed with visibility and credit, humility is a quiet
superpower. It doesn't shout. It doesn't strive to be the loudest voice
in the room. Humility listens. It makes space. It centers the
mission—not the ego. And in leadership, humility is often the thing
that separates those who manage from those who inspire.

To see this clearly, let's look at three leaders who embodied humility
not as a buzzword, but as a cornerstone of how they showed up in
the world.

1. Ray Dalio – Building a Culture on Transparency, Not Ego

Ray Dalio, the founder of Bridgewater Associates—the largest hedge
fund in the world—built his company on radical honesty paired with

extreme transparency. It sounds bold, even intimidating, but at the core of that system is humility.

Dalio openly admits he doesn't have all the answers.
He built processes so **everyone's insight matters**—whether they're an intern or an executive.

One of his most defining practices is the **Dot Collector**, a real-time tool that lets employees rate one another on attributes like thoughtfulness, humility, and logic. That system allowed team members to praise one another for silencing ego and working for the good of the collective.

He paired honesty with humility by **recording nearly every meeting** and making them accessible to everyone in the firm. He has been called out publicly by his staff—and instead of shutting it down, he welcomed it. Because he knew leadership wasn't about being right. It was about learning.

Dalio once said:

"If you're not failing, you're not pushing your limits, and if you're not pushing your limits, you're not maximizing your potential."

That's humility.
That's honesty.
That's leadership that invites others in.

2. Jim Sinegal and Costco – Deflecting Praise, Elevating Purpose

Costco co-founder Jim Sinegal is often praised for his leadership style—treating employees with dignity, offering fair wages, and creating a culture of trust. But one of his most defining qualities is his humility.

When union concerns arose in the early 2000s, Sinegal didn't respond defensively. He didn't gaslight. He didn't spin. He wrote an internal memo acknowledging the concerns and inviting dialogue, not denial.

In that memo he said:

"You can't say 'people are our most important product' and then treat them badly."

Sinegal cut through corporate hypocrisy with honesty and clarity. He reminded the company that values without behavior aren't values at all.

He went further:

"If you're a manager, teaching is 90 percent of your job. We hire because we can't do everything ourselves. If you're not prepared to teach, you just don't get it."

That wasn't a slogan.
It was a standard.

Sinegal emphasized that leadership is about developing others—not performing for them. He removed hierarchical distance not through policies, but through presence. He visited warehouses wearing the same badge as everyone else. He learned employees' names. He listened.

It would have been easy to flex numbers or parade benefits. But Sinegal chose humility. He knew his responsibility wasn't to win a debate—it was to honor the people who made his company possible.

That memo wasn't performative.
It was leadership in action.

3. Harry Kraemer – Leading with Self-Reflection

Harry Kraemer, former CEO of Baxter International and professor at Northwestern University's Kellogg School of Management, teaches that humility is the foundation of **values-based leadership**.

His daily discipline?
Fifteen minutes of self-reflection every night.

He journals—not about tasks or meetings—but about how he lived his values that day.

That requires humility.
It's easier to review your calendar than your character.

Kraemer teaches that if you're always talking and never reflecting, your leadership becomes a performance. But if you're willing to sit in silence and ask yourself hard questions, you evolve. You listen better. You lead better. You live better.

Each of these leaders showed, in different ways, that humility isn't weakness. It's wisdom.

It's a lesson I learned the hard way in my own leadership.
Good leaders resist the temptation to be the center of attention.
They don't thrive on superiority.
They use their platforms to elevate others, create safety, and build sustainable cultures.

Humility in leadership looks like:

- Listening more than speaking

- Seeking feedback instead of validation

- Sharing credit generously

- Owning mistakes publicly

- Deferring to expertise, even when it's not your own

It also means understanding the weight of influence.
As leaders, people watch what you celebrate and what you ignore.
Humble leaders celebrate team wins. They shine a light on people who rarely get it. They know leadership isn't about being impressive—it's about being effective.

And because they're secure in who they are, they can draw out hidden talent and extract the best their teams have to offer.

So if you find yourself in a room where everyone's looking to you for answers, **pause**.
Ask a question instead.
Make space for another voice.

This isn't about being "nice."
It's about unlocking ideas that would otherwise stay buried.

Most importantly, humility requires inward examination.
You must ask yourself:
What's guiding me—service, or self?

Because the best leaders aren't the ones who make everything about them.

They're the ones who remind everyone what's really worth showing up for.

REFLECTION EXERCISES

Think of a humble leader you know. List ten qualities about them you would like to emulate:

"I'm hungry for knowledge... to learn every day, to get brighter and brighter. That's what this world is about. You look at someone like Gandhi, and he glowed. Martin Luther King glowed. Muhammad Ali glowed. I think that's from being bright all the time, and trying to be brighter." — Jay-Z

CHAPTER 7 FAITH – A FOUNDATION FOR GROWTH

Humility prepares the heart for something deeper.
Once you quiet the ego, quiet the noise, and quiet the need to prove
yourself, you finally create space for the one force that makes true
transformation possible.

Faith.

Humility opens the door, but faith gives you the courage to walk
through it.
Humility says "I don't know everything."
Faith says "But I believe there's more for me."

After all the self-honesty…
After all the unlearning…
After all the leadership lessons…

You reach a point where growth requires something greater than
discipline, strategy, or talent.
It requires belief.

Not belief in perfection.
Not belief in circumstances.
Belief in possibility.

And that brings us to the next stage of the Butterfly Affect Framework.

Chapter 7: Faith – A Foundation for Growth

Without faith, it will be difficult to succeed in the Growth Phase of the Butterfly Affect Framework. Faith gives you the strength to keep going when everything around you tells you to quit. Faith sparks inspiration when the light at the end of the tunnel has flickered out. Faith becomes the foundation of the hope you need to dream, to build, to rise—especially when all you've ever known is instability.

I know this because faith was the lifeline that pulled me through the chaos.

When my mother finally divorced her abusive husband, it wasn't the ending of difficulty we all prayed for. It was just the beginning of another chapter of survival. We moved from one crisis to the next. She dabbled in drugs. We fell deeper into poverty. There were times when we were food insecure, living in an urban setting where hope seemed in short supply. Homelessness wasn't a season—it was a recurring storm.

My mother worked a series of menial jobs that drained her spirit and barely kept food on the table. We moved often, sleeping in unfamiliar rooms, packing and unpacking our lives in spaces that never felt like home. I remember asking friends to drop me off blocks away from where we lived, just so they wouldn't see the place we were staying. I checked over my shoulder to make sure they were gone before I walked the rest of the way.

There were months when we didn't have lights, gas, or running water at the same time. Sometimes we had electricity but no heat. Sometimes gas but no water. I remember the sting of winter nights with no heat and the shame of bathing from pots.

And in those moments, I made a quiet vow:

"When I grow up, this will not be my reality."

That wasn't fantasy—it was declaration. Speaking what didn't exist as though it did.

That's faith.

Hebrews 11:1 says,
"Now faith is the substance of things hoped for, the evidence of things not seen."
My present was dark, but my faith illuminated what my future could be.

But in the meantime, survival required creativity.

We didn't have a working stove, but we had a kerosene heater. My siblings and I huddled around it at night. One day I realized it could serve another purpose—it could cook food. I learned to fry eggs and warm meals on top of it so we didn't have to eat cold sandwiches.

And the bologna sandwiches?
I ate so many of them out of necessity that I haven't eaten one since.

Eventually we moved into a nicer home in a quiet neighborhood, and my aunt moved in with us. Even though we were still hungry some nights, her faith was abundant. She took us to church faithfully and planted seeds of Scripture and song deep into my soul.

Church dinners became my favorite meals—and sometimes the only hot ones. At first, I went to church for the food. But God had prepared something different for me.

My world began to expand.

My faith was activated in that little church. The music pulled me in, and soon I joined the choir. That's when I discovered a voice I didn't know I had. Singing gave me confidence, purpose, and belonging. I began to feel part of something bigger than the pain I came from.

I was surrounded by women of deep faith—godmothers, church mothers, aunties in the pews—women who spoke life over me when I felt invisible. They told me I was intelligent. They told me I was gifted. They told me God had plans for me. They told me what I was living wasn't the end of my story.

And I believed them.
Not because their words were fancy—but because **they were living proof.**

Faith doesn't always erase circumstances, but it gives you the strength to outlast them.

James 2:17 reminds us, **"Faith without works is dead."**
I didn't just hope things would change—I worked. I studied. I cooked. I learned how to stretch food, manage a home, take care of people. I became a leader long before I held a title. Faith fueled that fire.

I also became a leader in that little choir, taking the lead on songs that lifted people out of their pews and into praise.

As I matured, I realized something about leadership:
It is often forged in adversity.

It's easy to lead when everything is going well.
But how do you lead when the lights are off and the fridge is empty?
How do you lead when you're a teenager making dinner on a kerosene heater?
How do you lead when you're navigating trauma without therapy and heartbreak without help?

Faith made me a leader.

It taught me resilience.
It gave me vision.
It made me resourceful.

When I didn't have what I needed, faith helped me ask: **"What do I have?"**

I didn't have an oven, but I had a heater.
I didn't have groceries, but I had a neighbor who might share a can of something.
I didn't have stability, but I had a Savior.

That mindset shift—that growth—was only possible through the lens of faith.

Romans 5:3–4 says,
"Tribulation worketh patience; and patience, experience; and experience, hope."
Every hardship built something in me.
Every loss taught me empathy.
Every storm taught me how to find calm within myself—and help others find it too.

Great leaders don't fold under pressure.
They find solutions.
They leverage what they have.
They stay connected to something greater than the problem.

Faith does that.
It helps you look beyond the crisis and see possibility.

I've learned faith isn't just personal—it's organizational.
Churches thrive on it.
Movements are born from it.
Companies need it.
Teams rally because of it.

Because at its core, **faith is belief.**
And belief is contagious.

Habakkuk 2:2–3 teaches us to wait for the vision.
Faith builds patience—something every leader needs.
There are seasons where nothing seems to move.
Seasons where your prayers feel unanswered.
Seasons where your vision board seems to mock you.

That's when faith holds you steady.
That's when you revisit the vision and remind yourself why you
started.

Because when the vision speaks—**it speaks loud.**

My growth wasn't linear. I stumbled. I doubted. I cried. I questioned
God. But each time, I returned to faith. Not out of perfection, but out
of anchoring.

Anchored by Isaiah 40:31:
"They that wait upon the Lord shall renew their strength..."

Now, as a leader, I bring my whole self into every room:
the little girl who prayed for light,
the teenager who sang for strength,
and the woman who knows how to lead with grace—even when her
stomach is growling.

Faith was the bridge between acceptance and growth.
It helped me accept what was real without being imprisoned by it.
It allowed me to grieve what I didn't have while building what I needed.

Most of all, faith helped me grow—not just into a better version of myself, but into a woman who leads with vision, conviction, and compassion.

REFLECTION EXERCISES

It's essential to have a clear set of core values that align with your beliefs. These are not easy to form. They should be values you possess or strive for, and they should be non-negotiable. Write 3 "I believe" statements below:

I believe..

....

....

I believe..

....

....

I believe..

....

....

CHAPTER 8: THE COCOON OF GROWTH

We talked about humility earlier. But let's be clear: humility isn't a one-time checkpoint on the leadership journey. In the Butterfly Affect Framework, humility travels with us through every phase: Acceptance, Growth, and Transformation. And sometimes humility doesn't feel graceful or poetic. Sometimes humility feels like humiliation.

I know that kind.

I once carried my life in a garbage bag.

Not metaphorically, a literal black trash bag, stretched and torn at the edges from being dragged too long. It held my clothes, my shoes, and whatever dignity I could salvage. After church, I went from house to house asking if I could sleep on someone's couch or on a spare patch of carpet. Some said yes. Others said no. I wasn't angry. I was humiliated.

It's one thing to need help.
It's another to need it so deeply you have to ask for it out loud.

And still—I kept going.

I walked the streets with my eyes trained on the concrete, searching for loose quarters, nickels, and dimes. Fifty cents was gold back then. That was enough to ride the bus to school. If I didn't find enough, I walked. Miles. Rain or shine. Crying one day, singing to myself the next.

People talk about nervous breakdowns as if they are dramatic collapses. Mine didn't come with fireworks. It came quietly, in fatigue, frustration, and a kind of desperation that settles deep into your bones. But even then, I knew what I wanted. I knew education was my ticket forward. And I knew—deep in my bones, that my current reality was not my destiny.

So I kept showing up.

Church became my sanctuary. Not because my relationship with God was perfect, but because church gave me something my life didn't: rhythm. Consistency. Warmth. Sunday meals were sacred—not just spiritually, but literally. Sometimes they were the only real food I had all week. I didn't just go for the sermon. I went for the cornbread and greens. For the hospitality. For the sense of belonging in a room full of people who were singing through their struggle.

That's where I found my tribe.

We were a group of kids who didn't fit anywhere else: foster kids, kids with distracted parents, kids who drifted between homes. Kids like me. They called us "the Misfits," and we wore that name like armor. Not because we liked it, but because it reminded us that we were strongest together. We lifted each other up. We cracked jokes. We sang. We shared peanut butter sandwiches. We saved each other from collapsing under the weight of our circumstances.

Singing became my outlet. My therapy. My prayer. My declaration. Leading praise and worship gave me confidence nothing else could. When I stepped to the mic, the world faded. I wasn't the girl with a trash bag. I was a vessel. A voice. A reminder to myself that something holy was happening inside me—even on the days when my stomach growled or my shoes had holes.

Music helped me survive the humiliation.
It gave me breath when shame tried to choke me.
And slowly, I started to believe the words I was singing.

That God had a plan.
That joy was coming in the morning.
That my latter days would be greater than my former ones.

But growth didn't come just from surviving.

It came from curiosity and bravery—two qualities most people underestimate.

Many never grow because they lack one or both.
Curiosity whispers, "What if?"
What if I try?
What if I ask?
What if I go?
What if I dare?

Bravery is the muscle that lets you move through fear.
It's showing up again after humiliation.
It's auditioning again.
It's walking again.
It's believing again.

Most leaders never reach their potential because they confuse perfection with purpose. They believe they need all the answers before they begin. They think leadership is about certainty. But real leaders don't lead because they know everything—they lead because they are willing to learn.

Curiosity pushed me to read with a flashlight when the lights were off.
It made me join the choir even when I wasn't sure my voice was good.
It pushed me to apply for jobs I didn't think I'd get.
It made me dream bigger than the neighborhood I was born in.

Bravery carried me the rest of the way—through every audition, every scholarship application, every solo I sang with trembling hands. Bravery walked me to school with blisters on my heels. Bravery helped me believe I was a leader long before I felt like one.

Looking back now, I realize something vital:
None of those things broke me.
They stretched me.

They stretched my patience.
Stretched my resilience.
Stretched my imagination.
And stretching is what growth feels like.

You don't grow by staying comfortable.
You don't grow by avoiding risk.
You don't grow by waiting until you feel "ready."

Ready is a lie.

Most people aren't ready. They're just willing.
And willingness is what eventually becomes readiness.

Growth requires willingness to stretch beyond what should have broken you.
Willingness to forgive what hurt you.
Willingness to ask hard questions.
Willingness to tell the truth about what you've lived—and who you want to become.

That's the difference between stagnation and evolution:
Honesty.
Curiosity.
Bravery.

If you're in a season of humility—or humiliation, hear me: you are not alone.

Many of the strongest leaders I know have walked the same path.
They, too, carried their lives in trash bags.
They, too, asked strangers for couches.
They, too, walked until their legs ached and sang until their voices cracked.
And they kept going.

Because somewhere deep inside, they knew the pain was clearing space for something bigger.
They knew their current reality was not their final chapter.
They knew growth was not only possible, **it was promised.**

Your story isn't over.
Your brilliance hasn't peaked.
Your growth is already underway.

But it will require your curiosity.
It will demand your bravery.
And when those two show up, your growth becomes inevitable.

So lean in.
Ask the question.
Say yes.
Keep walking.
Keep singing.
Keep showing up.

Because your latter days?
They are already being written, and they are greater than anything you've left behind.

Growth stretches you, reshapes you, and asks you to become someone new.
But eventually, growth meets resistance. Expansion meets pressure. Vision meets reality. The cocoon gets tight. The stakes get high. The journey gets harder before it gets holy.

Because every evolution comes with weight.
Every elevation comes with heat.
Every breakthrough passes through pressure.

And that's where growth becomes grit, and grit becomes glory.

REFLECTION EXERCISES

Ready vs. Willing

Where in my life am I waiting to feel "ready" instead of deciding to be willing?

____

____

____

____

____

What's one area where I can commit to taking a step—even if I don't feel prepared?

____

____

____

____

____

What would it look like for me to stretch beyond what was meant to break me?

CHAPTER 9: HEAT, TIME, AND PRESSURE

If the cocoon teaches us anything, it's that growth is not always a beautiful process. It is pressure-filled. It is dark. It demands surrender—something most of us resist with every part of ourselves. Yet the cocoon is not a place of weakness; it is a chamber of extreme growth when we stop fighting it and allow the transformation to take root. You are not breaking down in this season; you are breaking open.

The Diamond Principle

Think about diamonds—one of the world's most valued and radiant treasures. We love their brilliance and the way they adorn us, signaling beauty, value, and refinement. But every diamond carries a story deeper than its shine. Long before it glitters, it begins as nothing more than carbon buried deep beneath the earth's surface. Down there, it is subjected to crushing pressure and blistering heat. Over long, unseen stretches of time, under conditions so extreme that most things would break, that carbon transforms into something magnificent.

The process is slow.
It is not gentle.
It demands endurance.

Leadership is no different.

Every great leader I've ever known has endured their carbon phase—seasons where the pressure is so intense it feels like the weight will collapse them. Times when the heat of responsibility and the squeeze of expectation make them question whether they were ever meant to lead at all. But those who emerge from these seasons with clarity, integrity, and depth—those are the diamonds among us. Not because they never cracked, but because the pressure forged them into something stronger and more brilliant.

Pressure exposes what we're made of, but it also refines us. It pushes out impurities, strips away ego, and aligns us with what actually matters. Leaders who don't try to escape pressure too soon become the ones with depth, wisdom, and unshakeable presence. They shine—not because life has been easy, but because they were willing to stay in the heat long enough to become who they were meant to be.

The Iron Principle

There is another everyday object that mirrors the leadership journey perfectly: the iron. An iron works by applying heat and pressure to remove wrinkles. What was once creased, crumpled, or disordered becomes smooth, sharp, and prepared—but only because it endured the heat.

Leaders experience the same process.
We are pressed by expectations.
Heated by decisions.
Stretched by challenges we didn't anticipate.

Our wrinkles show up as ego, insecurity, reactivity, indecision, avoidance, fear of conflict, poor communication, micromanagement, or the need to control everything. These wrinkles distort how we lead and how we are perceived.

And just like fabric under an iron, **heat reveals the wrinkles**.

A difficult team member highlights your need for control.
A failed project uncovers your discomfort with collaboration.
A confident peer surfaces your insecurity around sharing the spotlight.

These moments are not signs of failure. They are invitations.
Each wrinkle signals a part of your leadership that needs refinement.

A crisp shirt doesn't happen by accident.
Neither does a refined leader.

You are being ironed out for impact.
So when the heat rises, don't run.
That pressure is your polish in progress.

When the steam settles and the heat fades, what will remain is the version of you shaped not only by fire, but by faith, pressure, and persistence—and that version will be ready to lead.

The Cocoon Principle

If you are in a season of pressure, don't rush it. Don't curse it. Don't collapse beneath it. Surrender to it. Allow it to shape you. Allow it to refine you. Allow it to press out everything that is no longer essential, because growth isn't always about adding more— sometimes it's about letting go of what has been weighing you down.

My editor once shared a story that beautifully captures this principle. She bought her children a butterfly kit that came with an enclosure and six small caterpillars. The family watched each day as the caterpillars climbed to an artificial branch and spun their cocoons.

They were just days away from seeing the butterflies emerge and take flight.

But one afternoon, she left the enclosure within reach. Her toddlers "helped" the butterflies by prying open five of the six cocoons. Those five butterflies never flew. They died the next day. The only one who survived was the one whose cocoon was left untouched.

Why?

Because the butterfly needs the struggle. Breaking through the cocoon builds its wings. Even after emerging, it hangs from the branch, pumping and flapping its wings to strengthen them before ever attempting to fly. The struggle is not just part of the process—it is the process.

Leaders are no different.

If someone pulls you out too soon, you never develop strength.
If you avoid the struggle, you bypass wisdom.
If you escape the pressure, your wings never form.

Some leaders never gain depth because they have never survived anything that demanded growth.

Real growth requires grit. It is pressure turned into purpose. So if you feel like you're unraveling, good. Stay there. Let yourself break open. Let the old identity dissolve. The cocoon is not a prison—it is a passage.

And on the other side, you will not emerge as who you were.
You will emerge as who you were meant to be.

That is growth.
That is resilience.
That is leadership with wings.

REFLECTION EXERCISES

Let's talk about the hard things. Kindly describe a previous experience that played a significant role in imparting a valuable lesson. Then compare those two present struggles that, although hard, might be working in your favor.

CHAPTER 10: THE GROWTH CYCLE OF A LEADER

Heat shapes authenticity. But responsibility reveals capacity.

When I stepped into my first official manager role, I did not just inherit a title. I inherited a team in survival mode. And survival is a language I speak fluently.

The unit was struggling across nearly every measurable metric. Engagement was low.

Outcomes were inconsistent.

Trust was fragile.

The team had history—long tenure, loyalty to a previous leader, fatigue from change, and frustration that had quietly settled into the culture.

They were not defiant.

They were tired.

The moment I recognized that they were operating from survival, something in me activated.

I knew that posture.

I knew what it felt like to focus only on making it through the day. To conserve energy.

To protect trust.

To brace for disappointment.

Survival narrows vision.

It makes you cautious, guarded, reactive. But survival also holds strength—resilience, instinct, endurance. The question was not how to control a struggling unit. The question was how to shift them from surviving to stretching.

I will never forget my first large leadership meeting. Results were projected on the screen, department by department. And then—my unit.

At the bottom of the scorecard. There is nothing theoretical about seeing your name next to the lowest metrics in the building.

It gets real quickly.

In that moment, I felt two instincts rise.

One familiar.

One mature.

The familiar instinct was survival—defend, explain, distance myself from the data. After all, I had just taken over. The mature instinct was stewardship—own it, lead it, stretch through it. Growth happens in that split second between reaction and response.

I took a breath.

Less of me.

More of Thee.

Because this was not about protecting my pride.
It was about elevating a team.
The unit was in survival mode—and so was I for a moment.

But I knew something they did not yet see. Survival is a stage.

It is not a destiny. If I led from fear, they would stay guarded.

If I led from clarity, they could rise. So I chose clarity.

We confronted the data without shame.

We named the gaps without blame. We set standards without apology.

And I did something critical—I trusted them. Not blindly.

Intentionally.

Long tenure was not the problem. Misalignment was.

These were capable professionals who had adapted to survive.

My role was not to replace them. It was to reawaken them.

I met with them individually. I listened.

I asked what had dimmed their belief.
I asked what they needed from leadership that they had not received.

And then I raised the bar. Survival lowers standards to conserve energy.
Stretching raises standards to expand capacity.
That shift is uncomfortable.

There were tense conversations. Moments of resistance.

Days when progress felt microscopic.

But something began to change. Ownership increased.
Language shifted from "they" to "we."

Accountability became shared.
The same team that once sat at the bottom of the scorecard climbed—
steadily and deliberately—into the top decile in under a year.

The metrics mattered. But the most important shift was not on the
spreadsheet or department scorecard. It was trust.

They trusted me to lead. Not because I controlled them. Because I
understood them.

Because I did not shame their survival—I honored it.

And then I invited them beyond it.

That is the growth cycle of a leader. Pressure reveals survival instincts.
Responsibility invites stretch. Stewardship creates transformation.

When you recognize survival in others, you have a choice.
You can exploit it. You can ignore it. Or you can lead them through it.

The stretch in this season was not about learning new technical skills.

It was about expanding my capacity to hold tension without shrinking.

To stay steady when results lagged.

To believe before the data reflected belief.

To lead not for applause, but for elevation.

And here is what I learned: the moment you step into greater

responsibility, your survival story will try to reappear.

Not to defeat you. To test you.

Growth is choosing not to lead from old wounds.

It is choosing to lead from earned wisdom.

If you are stepping into a new assignment right now

and the numbers look daunting, the culture feels fragile,

or the expectations feel heavy—pause.

Ask yourself: am I reacting from survival, or responding from
stewardship?

Because the stretch is not just about improving performance.

It is about expanding capacity—yours and the team you're leading.

And when you steward power wisely—when you stretch

instead of shrink—you do more than change metrics.

You change paradigms.

You change momentum.

You create opportunity.

And opportunity, when seized, becomes a trail others can follow.

REFLECTION EXERCISES

The Stretch Goal Challenge

Growth isn't just surviving—it's stretching.

You've heard me say it: *"Stretch beyond what was meant to break you."* Let's make that real.

A stretch goal is not something safe and small that you know you'll tick off next week. It's bigger. Bolder. It's the goal that makes your stomach flip a little because it demands a new level of you. It pushes you past the edges of what's comfortable. And that's where transformation happens.

Right now, let's set a stretch goal in one of three powerful arenas:

Leadership
Career
Personal Development

Step 1: Pick Your Arena

Ask yourself:

- In my leadership, where do I want to grow or show up differently?

- In my career, what feels just out of reach but deeply important?

- In my personal life, where am I ready to become more of who I'm meant to be?

Pick the one that resonates most today.

Step 2: Dream the Bold Vision

Finish this sentence:

"I am growing toward this one big thing..."

Examples:

- **Leadership:** *"I want to lead a team workshop to build psychological safety and trust."*

- **Career:** *"I want to apply for a director-level position, even though I'm terrified I'm not ready."*

- **Personal Development:** *"I want to start therapy to work through trauma."*

Step 3: Get Specific

Turn your vision into a clear, measurable goal.

Instead of:

"I want to be a better leader."

Say:

"I will schedule monthly one-on-one meetings with each team member to build connection and trust, starting next month."

Instead of:

"I want to change my career."

Say:

"I will apply to three roles in my target industry by March 1."

Instead of:

"I want to work on myself."

Say:

"I will join a weekly therapy group and attend at least six sessions."

Step 4: Check the Stretch Factor

Ask yourself:

- Does this goal make me feel slightly nervous—but excited?
- Will it require me to learn, risk, or grow in new ways?
- Does it feel like it would make me proud—even if it's hard?

If it feels too easy, **stretch it further.** It should give you a twinge of hesitation.

Step 5: Write Your "Why"

A stretch goal needs fuel. Write your reason:

"I want this because…"

Examples:

- **Leadership:** *"I want my team to trust me enough to tell me the truth—even the hard truths."*

- **Career:** *"I want to do work that excites me and honors my potential."*

- **Personal Development:** *"I want to stop living out the patterns that keep me small."*

Step 6: Name Your First Step

Every stretch goal begins small. Write the **very first step** you'll take in the next 48 hours.

Examples:

- **Leadership:** Email my team to schedule the first round of one-on-ones.

- **Career:** Update my resume and ask two colleagues for feedback.

- **Personal Development:** Research local therapy groups or coaches and make one inquiry.

Step 7: Create Accountability

Don't keep your stretch goal a secret. Share it with someone you trust—a friend, mentor, coach, or even your journal. Set a check-in date.

Because what you say out loud is what you start to believe.

Reflection: Imagine the Win

Write a few sentences capturing that future vision. Let it pull you forward.

Here's an **example**:

- **Arena:** Career

- **Stretch Goal:** "I will launch my own business by December 1."

- **Why:** "Because I want to build generational wealth and serve people with my story."

- **First Step:** "Block two hours this week to outline my business plan."

- **The Win:** "I did it. My business is running and I have 12 new clients."

One final truth:

Growth isn't waiting for you to feel ready. It's waiting for you to say yes—even while your voice shakes.

So pick your arena. Set your stretch goal. And stretch beyond what was meant to break you.

CHAPTER 11: THE POWER OF OPPORTUNITY

There are so many moments in life where your bravery and curiosity intersect—and when they do, they form a key. A key that opens doors to something bigger than you ever imagined. One of the greatest doors that key can unlock is opportunity.

Opportunity is not a myth. It's not reserved for the lucky, the privileged, or the perfectly prepared. Opportunity is everywhere. But only visible to those who know how to see it. Even as a child, I noticed early that leadership was a gift in me. I could spot a need before others realized it was there. I saw strengths in people they didn't see in themselves. That instinct, seeing possibility in places others overlook, is one of the earliest signs of a leader who knows how to recognize opportunity.

Most people breeze right past their big break, their defining moment, because they don't recognize it when it shows up. Why? Because opportunity doesn't always come dressed in certainty. It hardly ever arrives at a convenient time. Often, it shows up disguised as fear, inconvenience, challenge, or risk.

And that's the first truth: **opportunity is often frightening.**

But here's what great leaders understand: this is the fun part. Growth lives in discomfort. Transformation begins at the edge of what feels familiar. Without fear, without the stretch, without that internal shake, we would never leave what feels safe. And nothing extraordinary ever grows in the comfort zone.

Opportunity rarely announces itself with a sign that reads: **This Is It.** Sometimes it whispers. Sometimes it's wrapped in chaos. Sometimes it appears to be a loss before it becomes a gain. Adversity, though painful, has a strange way of opening doors. Growing up, I often found myself in leadership roles — leading choirs, becoming a top JROTC officer despite being homeless, and guiding youth groups — not because I demanded to lead, but because people trusted my clarity and conviction. Even when life was unstable, opportunity kept showing up disguised as responsibility.

To recognize opportunity, *you need the right glasses.*

Leaders must learn to see the world through what I call **opportunity lenses**. These aren't rose-colored glasses. They're purpose-colored glasses. They help you examine what others fear and find possibility. They help you look at what others reject and see potential. They give you the faith to take a step when everyone else is frozen.

Just like someone who is nearsighted needs glasses to see things far away, many leaders suffer from mental nearsightedness. They're so focused on today's problems and immediate crises that they lose sight of the long-term vision. Others are the opposite; they're farsighted. They dream big but overlook what's unfolding right in front of them.

Effective leadership requires **bifocal vision**, the ability to zoom in and zoom out. You must care deeply about what's happening right now: today's staffing, today's budget, today's patient experience. At the same time, you must lift your gaze and prepare your team for what's ahead. Leadership is a constant balancing act between managing the moment and shaping the future.

This is management bifocal vision: part analyst, part visionary. You deal with today while designing tomorrow. And if you're not actively developing the people around you, you're missing half the job. Your team should evolve as much as you do.

As a leader, you must build capacity, not just manage it. This involves identifying hidden potential, mentoring your team, and placing people in roles that allow them to grow and stretch. It means holding space for brainstorming, asking deeper questions, and giving people projects that challenge them. One of the greatest gifts you can give your organization is a team that's not just effective but inspired.

Let me say that again for the readers in the back:
One of the greatest gifts you can give your organization is a team that's not just effective but inspired!

Developing your team isn't about control. It's about cultivating growth. It isn't micromanaging; it's mentoring. Leadership is not rooted in perfection but in progress. Invite your team into the vision. Call them to rise with you. Coach them through the discomfort of new skills. Celebrate their creativity and resilience. Let them witness your process—and share theirs.

Consider Oprah Winfrey. Fired from her first job as a news anchor because she was "too emotional," "too dramatic," "not the right look." But Oprah saw an opportunity where others saw rejection. The very qualities they criticized, empathy, vulnerability, depth, became her superpowers. She didn't fight for someone else's table. She built her own.

Or Sara Blakely, founder of Spanx. She sold fax machines door-to-door. No investors. No connections. No fancy degree. Just an idea—and an opportunity lens. She used her own savings, studied patent law, and pitched her product directly to department stores. Her bravery met her curiosity. Spanx was born. Now she's one of the youngest self-made female billionaires in the world.

Or Howard Schultz. He grew up in public housing, but when he saw how coffee shops in Italy brought people together, he saw something others missed. His opportunity lens wasn't about coffee. It was about connections. Starbucks became a global movement.

One of my earliest lessons in opportunity lenses came when I became a charge nurse. Our scheduling system was chaotic, with constant holes, stressed staff, and declining morale. I saw an opportunity where others saw frustration. When I asked to help with scheduling, my manager said yes. I built trust, aligned strengths, stabilized the workflow, and improved patient care. That was opportunity inside a problem — maybe one of the first times I realized leadership is simply the willingness to step into the gap.

So many of us miss our moment because we're waiting for certainty. Let me say this plainly: **certainty is a privilege you earn later.**

In the beginning, all you have is a whisper, a tug, a quiet question you can't shake. That's opportunity trying to introduce itself before you're convinced it's real. If you wait for fear to vanish, you'll miss it. If you wait to feel fully ready, you'll miss it. If you wait for permission, you'll miss it.

The doorway to change rarely comes with certainty; it comes with a nudge, and your willingness to follow it.

Bravery means saying yes while your hands are still shaking. Curiosity means exploring what's possible before anyone hands you a roadmap.
Opportunity happens when you respond with both.

Some of the greatest opportunities in my life looked nothing like blessings. They looked like heartbreak. A broken-down car. A late bill notice. A failed marriage. But on the other side of each of those moments came something better, a new connection, a new idea, a new version of me.

How will you know what you're good at if you don't explore the opportunities that come your way?

You won't.

The best leaders are explorers. They say yes to the internship, even if it's unpaid. They sign up for the class, even if they're the oldest student in the room. They apply for the promotion, even if they don't meet every requirement. They understand this truth:

You don't discover your gifts by playing it safe.
You discover them by stretching. By experimenting.
By being willing to look foolish while you learn.

Opportunity is everywhere. The question is:
Will you see it? Will you trust it? Will you walk through the door?

Remember: some doors are new because you've reached a new level. Others were always there, but transformation sharpened your awareness enough to see them finally. Opportunity expands as you grow. As your vision expands, so does your influence.

REFLECTION EXERCISES

Say yes!

Opportunity is also generous. It's not a one-time offer. It keeps circling back. It knocks more than once. But you must stay open. You must stay available.

Here's what that looks like in real life:

- You say yes to the meeting.

- You speak up in the room.

- You volunteer for the project.

- You start the side hustle.

- You introduce yourself.

These little moments become the pivot points of your life. They become the chapters you tell later when people ask, "How did you get here?"

The truth is, you're already standing near something that could change your life. However, you must have the courage to look more closely.

So many people don't lead because they never allow themselves to stretch. They're still waiting for a mentor to validate them, a boss to notice them, a system to promote them. However, opportunity doesn't rely solely on external validation.

It waits on your internal decision.

You decide if you'll leap. You decide if you'll explore. You decide if you'll put the glasses on and see the world not as it is, but as it could be.

That's leadership. That's growth. That's the spark that changes everything.

So ask yourself today:

- What have I been too afraid to try?

- Where have I been waiting for clarity instead of creating it?

- What opportunity might be hiding inside this problem?

Because yes, opportunity can be frightening. But it can also be **fun**.

And if you're not having any fun yet, maybe it's because you're still clinging to certainty. Let go. Be curious. Be brave.

Say yes.

And let opportunity do what it does best: change everything.

CHAPTER 12 – LEARNING TO STRETCH

Many leaders fail to grow beyond their current level because they believe their current approach is effective. And it might be—for now. Their numbers look decent. Their team hasn't revolted. Their supervisor isn't complaining. But bad leadership, even when temporarily effective, is never a formula for long-term influence. It isn't sustainable. It isn't scalable. And more importantly, it isn't transformational.

Some leaders aren't stuck because they lack vision or talent; they're stuck because they've hardened. Over time, they develop a kind of internal rigidity that renders them unable to evolve. Their thinking becomes fixed. Their responses become predictable. They lose the flexibility required to navigate today's relentless pace of change.

Yet **flexibility is the hallmark of enduring leadership**.

Rigid leaders struggle to adapt to new personalities, emerging technologies, shifting generational expectations, and the ever-changing landscape of modern work. They default to a single leadership style regardless of context. They cling to control. They micromanage. Or worse—they withdraw. When confronted with conflict or complexity, they react instead of reflect. Some erupt. Others retreat. Many disengage.

But leadership, in its truest form, demands adaptability. It demands emotional pliability and intellectual openness. The leaders who thrive are the ones who remain soft enough to bend without breaking—and wise enough to understand that evolution is not a threat, but a necessity.

Here's what inflexibility looks like in real time: a new hire questions an outdated process, and the rigid leader hears it as disrespect. A team member offers a creative solution, and the leader interprets it as a challenge to their authority. A crisis hits, and instead of reimagining and rallying, the leader spirals into panic, paralysis, or hyper-control.

This is where the metaphor of taffy becomes powerful.

At first glance, a lump of taffy is dense and unyielding—hard to bite into, impossible to shape, resistant to change. But in the hands of the candy maker—through steady pulling, folding, heating, and airing—it transforms. It stretches. It softens. It becomes pliable, responsive, and ready for whatever comes next.

Leadership is no different. Without intentional stretching through feedback, discomfort, conflict, and change, we stay hardened. We resist what could reshape us. But when we allow discomfort to work on us, we become leaders capable of guiding with flexibility, humanity, and endurance.

Stretching is uncomfortable. It demands a willingness to be reshaped. And yet without that tension—without the necessary pull—you remain a heavy, hardened version of yourself. Not because it's who you truly are, but because you have chosen not to move. Growth asks something of you. Refusing to stretch is not strength, it's resistance disguised as safety.

Every leader you admire has been stretched. Each has been pulled through seasons of doubt, crisis, transition, failure, loss, and reinvention. These moments didn't define them by what they endured—they defined them by how they responded. Rather than breaking, they allowed themselves to bend.

Stretching beyond what was meant to break you doesn't mean ignoring the pain. It means honoring it. It means letting the experience soften what needs softening and sharpen what needs growth. It means allowing adversity to expand your capacity for empathy, creativity, vision, and compassion.

You were never meant to lead from resistance.
You were meant to lead from resilience.

Not the kind of resilience that hardens you, but the kind that humbles you. The kind that keeps your heart open, your mind flexible, and your purpose clear—even when the pressure mounts.

Resilient leaders stay curious. They ask, *"What can I learn from this?"* instead of *"Why is this happening to me?"* They are brave—not because they never feel insecure, but because insecurity doesn't stop them from showing up. They're pliable. They adapt to change instead of resisting it. They stretch with it. They grow through it.

And here it is:
If you won't stretch, you can't grow.

Let's go back to the taffy for a moment.
The candy maker pulls and folds it not to weaken it, but to strengthen it. The stretching introduces air. As it's worked—pulled, aerated, and reshaped—it becomes soft, elastic, and usable. Without that process, taffy remains a brick: dense, immovable, unusable.

So, it is with leadership.

Without the stretch of uncomfortable conversations, you remain rigid.
Without the fold of self-reflection, there is no pliability.
And without pliability, there is no sustained growth.

Leaders who stretch beyond what was meant to break them tend to do a few things consistently:

1. They embrace change rather than resist it.

2. They value feedback, even when it stings, because they know growth requires it.

3. They invest in learning, even when it exposes their blind spots.

4. They lead with vulnerability, not just vision.

These leaders are agile. They bend without breaking. They adapt without losing their center. They remain relevant, trusted, and impactful in times of change.

Contrast this with leaders who refuse to stretch. Their teams walk on eggshells. Innovation stagnates. Culture decays. Morale plummets. And eventually, even if they keep their title, they lose their influence.

The very tension you fear may be the force that shapes your next level of growth. This isn't about lowering standards or abandoning boundaries. Great leadership still requires clarity about what's acceptable and what isn't. But you cannot inspire people if you don't invite them into the vision. When leadership becomes a one-way street, "my way or the highway", you may find your team choosing the highway.

And when they do, you're left carrying a vision alone or scrambling to rebuild what could have grown through shared investment.

Maybe you grew up believing you weren't enough. Maybe rejection taught you to protect instead of risk. Maybe one failure convinced you to lead from fear. Those experiences were real. They left marks. But they don't have to dictate your leadership story.

Like taffy, you can become pliable and strong, but only if you allow the process to work on you. The pulling, the stretching, the tension, it's not there to break you. It's there to shape you into someone who can lead with resilience and flexibility.

Leadership is not a monument you build once, climb on top of, and admire for the rest of your career.
Leadership is a movement, a dynamic, evolving force that invites you to participate in its unfolding. Not with control, but with surrender. Not with certainty, but with willingness. Not by staying rigid, but by learning to stretch.

Because when you do, you become the kind of leader people trust, not because you have all the answers, but because you've done the inner work to stay flexible, human, and open.

Stretching makes room.
Room for new ideas. Room for new strength. Room for new versions of yourself that could never have survived in the tight, rigid spaces you once occupied.

But stretching is only the beginning.

Because once you open yourself to growth, once you allow discomfort to reshape you, you step into a new phase of leadership. A phase where you're not just being stretched… you're being shaped. Molded. Positioned. Elevated.

Stretching prepares you.
Shaping transforms you.

And that's where we're headed next.

Stretch- **Accept**.

Become- **Grow**.

Lead-**Transform**.

REFLECTION EXERCISES

So, how do you become a leader who stretches?

Start with self-awareness. Identify the areas where you've become inflexible. Maybe it's the way you handle stress. Maybe it's your refusal to delegate. Maybe it's the way you dismiss ideas from younger or less experienced team members.

Then, begin the intentional practice of stretching.

- Ask for feedback from those who report to you.

- Sit with discomfort instead of avoiding it.

- Let yourself be wrong. And learn out loud.

Growth Toolkit:

Trying new things opens up new opportunities. Even if you are seasoned leader, there is always something new to discover. Take a look at the suggestions below and choose one to try tomorrow.

10 First-Time" Actions for Seasoned Leaders

1. Call Someone Just to Thank Them-No Agenda Instead of· emailing or texting, pick up the phone and say:
I'm not calling for a favor or a project. I just wanted you to know how much I appreciate what you bring to the team."

For many leaders, *pure gratitude without business talk* is completely new territory.

2. Sit Silently in a Meeting—On Purpose

Don't speak unless asked. Observe body language. Let others drive the conversation. Write down insights about how the team functions without your voice.

Ask a Direct Report: "What's One Thing I Do That Makes Your Job More Challenging?"

This is next-level vulnerability and it might blow open blind spots you've never noticed.

3. Share One Personal Failure in a Meeting
Pick a story you've never told before. Let people see your humanity. Then connect it to a leadership lesson.

5. Block Two Hours in Your Calendar for "Thinking Time"—and Actually No Meetings—and Keep It
No meetings. No emails. Just space to brainstorm, reflect, or dream without interruption. Leaders rarely give themselves permission to *not produce*.

6. Let Someone Else Make the Final Decision
On a decision you'd normally own, tell a team member:

"I trust your judgment. I'll support whatever you choose."

7. Admit You're Overwhelmed to Your Team

Instead of always being the strong one, say:

"I'm feeling stretched thin right now. I'm going to lean on you all more this week."

8. Learn One Thing About Each Person's Life Outside Work
Ask your team questions like: "What's something you're passionate about outside of work?" Then write it down and remember it.

People feel seen when leaders care about their *whole* selves.

9. Cancel a Meeting That Has Outlived its Usefulness

Identify one recurring meeting that drains energy. Announce:

"We're freeing up this hour. Let's all use it for focused work or rest."

10. Give the Spotlight to Someone Else Entirely

Instead of leading the next presentation, introduce a junior team member to share insights or results.

Sit quietly and let them shine.

CHAPTER 13: DEVELOP YOUR VISION

After you learn to stretch—to soften, to bend, to evolve, you step into a new dimension of leadership. Stretching prepares you. But vision directs you.

Because what good growth is if you don't know where you're heading?

That's where this chapter begins.

Let me talk straight: if you're leading anything—a team, a business, a household, or even just yourself—you need vision. Not the pretty, corporate buzzword kind. **Real vision.** The kind you can write down, stick on your fridge, whisper in prayer, and come back to when the world knocks you off balance.

There's a reason Scripture in Habakkuk says, *"Write the vision, and make it plain…"*
It's not about fancy language or poetic phrasing.
It's about clarity. Simplicity. Direction.
If you can't explain your vision in a way that someone else could run with it, you're not clear enough yet.

Many leaders remain stuck because they're too busy surviving today to think about tomorrow. They're putting out fires, juggling crises, reacting to everything, and assuming vision is a luxury for people who have time. But here's the truth: **vision is what fuels your endurance.** It's what steadies you when fatigue sets in. It's what pushes you forward when every part of you wants to quit. Vision reminds you what the fight is for.

I've lived through seasons when my vision felt like a punchline—when I was moving my belongings in trash bags, when nothing in my present looked anything like the dreams I had in my heart. Still, somewhere beneath the exhaustion and uncertainty, I held onto a quiet conviction: **my story wasn't finished.**

That's the power of vision.

Here's what I learned:

Speak your vision out loud, even if you feel silly, even if your voice trembles, even if you're the only one who believes it.

Write it down, even if it feels small. **Make it plain.** Don't keep it locked up in your mind. Put it on paper. Paper makes it real. Paper makes it accountable. Paper makes it measurable.

And keep it where you can see it. Your vision must be visible.
Put it on your mirror.
On your wall.
On your phone's lock screen.
Make it a part of your daily rhythm.

And you need people around you who help keep you accountable, people who applaud you and *pause* you. The ones who celebrate your wins but also ask, "Are you actually working toward the goal you keep talking about?" **Accountability is vision's guardrail.**

Too often, leaders don't speak their vision because of shame. Shame about how far they must go.

Shame about dreaming big when their present looks small.
Shame about failing publicly.

But silence kills dreams.
Releasing shame resurrects them.

There is no shame in wanting more.
There is no shame in growing.
There is no shame in declaring where you're headed before you've arrived.

Vision doesn't have to be perfect—just honest.
Write what you know today:

- How you want people to feel around you

- What kind of leader you want to be

- What impact you want to make

- What legacy you want to leave

Then be patient with it. Vision takes time. Sometimes it feels like nothing is happening. But trust **it's working beneath the surface.** One day, it will speak for itself. And when it finally speaks, it won't just carry you forward. It will carry the people who have been quietly watching you, too.

So if you're tired, afraid, or stuck in a season that feels like pure survival, **don't** retreat. Don't fold. Don't minimize your dreams.

Keep writing.
Keep speaking.
Keep believing.

Your vision is already taking shape, even if you can't see it yet. And eventually, **it will speak louder than you ever imagined.**

REFLECTION EXERCISES

Transformation Readiness Checklist

☐ **I'm willing to tell the truth about where I really am.**
Not just the highlight reel, but the mess, the mistakes, the hidden fears.

☐ **I'm open to letting go of old identities.**
Even the ones that protected me or made me feel important.

☐ **I'm prepared to feel uncomfortable.**
Because growth often feels awkward before it feels amazing.

☐ **I'm ready to ask for help.**
I know I don't have to do this alone.

☐ **I believe my story isn't over.**
There's still more of me to discover and more of my purpose to unfold.

☐ **I'm willing to change how I think, speak, and act.**
Transformation requires new habits   not just new hopes.

☐ **I know I deserve a life beyond survival.**
I want to thrive, not just exist.

☐ **I'm committed to small daily actions.**
I understand transformation happens one step at a time.

☐ **I'm curious about what's possible.**
I'm willing to explore new paths, even if I feel uncertain.

☐ **I'm ready to invest in myself.**

My time. My energy. My resources. I'm worth it.

Count your checks.

- **8-10 checks:** You're primed for transformation. Let's fly.

- **5-7 checks:** You're closer than you think. Pick one area to focus on right now.

- **1-4 checks:** Don't worry. Transformation isn't off the table—but start smaller. Go back to honesty and stretching before you push into full change.

Because transformation isn't a destination. It's a process.

And the leader you're becoming is worth every step.

"The 7 Steps to Transformation:

Dream it.

Envision it.

Think it.

Grow it.

Become it.

Live it.

OWN it."

— *Germany Kent*

CHAPTER 14: WINGS OF TRANSFORMATION

Coming out of the Growth Phase requires more than stretching, learning, and adapting. At some point, growth asks for something deeper. It asks you to become someone new. That is the beginning of transformation.

Transformation isn't a magic switch you flip.
It's a process you commit to.
It's sweat. It's trial and error. It's looking at yourself in the mirror and deciding that you're willing to dig deeper, stretch further, and rise beyond who you've been.
At the heart of transformation is one critical question:

What drives you?

Finding what drives you isn't always obvious. It's not printed on your birth certificate. You discover it inside your own story—inside the moments that stirred something in you. The losses that broke your heart. The work that made you feel alive. The moments when your pulse kicked up and your spirit whispered, *this matters*.

For me, I have always been a giver. If I found a quarter, *we* found a quarter. I remember searching parking lots with my best friend for pennies and nickels, gathering just enough to buy a bag of chips. Back then, a bag of chips wasn't half air—you could feed two or three kids. We squeezed every bag to find the fullest one. We were

strategic. We were resourceful.
And when we opened a bag of Vitner's Cheese Chips and found one giant chip inside, we didn't cry or complain. We broke it apart and shared it equally. That was who we were.

Later that day, my mother came home with a multipack of chips and gave each of us our own bag. Little moments like that shaped my faith. They taught me that generosity, hard work, and hope have a way of coming full circle. And the next day? We were right back out looking for change. Because transformation isn't a one-time act. It's consistency. It's effort. It's believing that small, faithful steps lead to extraordinary outcomes.

Transformation is continual personal growth.
It's refusing to settle for who you were yesterday. It's staying open to new information, new people, and new experiences—even when they scare you.

Transformation requires vulnerability. You cannot change without admitting that some parts of you must change. That truth alone stops many leaders from evolving. They fear that acknowledging flaws will make them appear weak. But the opposite is true:

Honesty makes you relatable.

Relatability makes you trustworthy.
And trust is the foundation of real influence.

People follow leaders who don't pretend to have it all together. People trust leaders who show how they've grown and who are still growing.

A major part of transformation is learning from your failures. We avoid the word *failure* as if it's fatal. But failure isn't death—it's data. It's feedback. It's direction. Some of my greatest breakthroughs came from my biggest disappointments. In those low, uncertain moments, I discovered what I was really made of. I saw my

resilience. My creativity. My ability to pivot when Plan A fell apart. I learned how to rise when everything around me suggested I should fall.
Those moments didn't break me, they revealed me.

Transformation also requires paying attention to your emotional responses. What makes your heart race? What subjects make you sit up straighter? What work makes you lose track of time? These signals are not random; they are spiritual breadcrumbs leading you toward your purpose.

True transformation gives you permission to dream bigger than your circumstances. As a kid carrying my belongings in trash bags, I never could have imagined leading teams, standing on stages, or writing books. But deep down, I believed I was meant for more. That belief—flickering but persistent—fueled the choices I made, even when fear whispered otherwise.

Transformation doesn't happen in isolation. The relationships around you shape it. Who are you walking with? Are they stretching you toward your potential or tethering you to old patterns? Growth sometimes requires distance—not out of arrogance, but out of alignment. Protecting your journey doesn't mean abandoning love; it means prioritizing purpose. And this is where transformation expands into something bigger than yourself.
Transformation becomes mentorship.

Leaders committed to transformation understand that growth is both personal and relational. They see potential in others and create space for it to rise. They teach. They mentor. They build environments where others step into their own strength. When transformation is rooted in purpose, it doesn't stay contained; it becomes contagious.

Transformation Lived Out: The Power of Lifting Others

Nobody becomes who they are alone. Not really. Someone, somewhere, held a door open, whispered your name in a room full of opportunity, or believed in you before you believed in yourself. That's mentorship. It isn't glamorous. It isn't perfect. But it is one of the purest expressions of transformed leadership.

As doors opened for me, doors that once felt locked tight, I realized something important: they weren't meant to close behind me. They became invitations to hold space for someone who would come after me. That's when leadership becomes legacy.

Early in my career, I thought leadership was about proving myself. About mastering the role. About carrying weight. But leadership rooted in transformation says:

"If I rise, you rise too."

Mentorship isn't about cloning yourself or controlling someone else's journey. It's about giving them tools, perspective, and space to grow into who *they* were meant to become.

I think about my early nursing days, the pressure, the uncertainty, the quiet fear that everyone else knew the handbook except me. Once I found my footing, I knew I didn't want to be the only one who made it through that door. I started assigning small projects to team members, quiet, intentional opportunities for them to lead.

People rose.
Not because I pushed them, but because someone finally saw them.

Some of the most powerful mentoring doesn't happen in formal programs. It happens in hallways. On late-night shifts. In passing conversations where someone says, "I'm overwhelmed," and you answer, "Here's what helped me."

Mentorship multiplies what transformation started.
It's not just about your wings, it's about helping someone else discover theirs.

I once worked with a young nurse who had brilliant ideas but a hesitant, apologetic voice. I told her about the years I spent practicing in the mirror, rehearsing courage until it felt natural. Little by little, she began speaking. First, a sentence. Then a question. Then a confident contribution in a meeting. Watching her own voice felt like watching someone take flight.

That's the ripple effect of transformed leadership:
You don't just rise—you raise.

The highest expression of mentorship is when it crosses lines, race, age, gender, and background, because transformation grows deeper when it disrupts old divisions and invites everyone to rise.

Mentorship requires surrender, too. You can guide, but you can't control outcomes. You can teach, but you must release. You can offer wisdom, but you can't walk someone else's path for them.

Some doors were never meant for you to stay in.
They were meant for you to hold open.

When leaders understand this, when they use their transformation not just for themselves, but for the transformation of others, cultures shift. Influence multiplies. Futures change.

The greatest leaders don't just carry their own dreams. They help others carry theirs.

Mentorship is transformation with purpose.
It's leadership with wings.

Transformation in the World: Lessons from Leaders

One of the most compelling stories of transformation in modern healthcare leadership that I've heard is that of Michael Dowling, the former CEO of Northwell Health. Growing up in rural Ireland in extreme poverty, working odd jobs, even as a janitor, to support his

family, he rose to lead New York's largest health system. His leadership wasn't powered by ambition alone—it was fueled by purpose. He carried the lessons of his early struggles into every boardroom and initiative, building a culture that centered on access, dignity, innovation, and social responsibility.
That's transformation: turning personal history into collective progress. Turning pain into purpose.

Or consider Oprah Winfrey. From a childhood marked by trauma and poverty to becoming one of the most influential women in global history, she didn't just change her own life—she transformed countless others by helping them see what was possible for themselves.

Transformation isn't reserved for CEOs or celebrities.
It shows up in everyday choices:
— going back to school at 40
— scheduling your first therapy appointment
— forgiving someone who never apologized
— applying for the job that intimidates you
— speaking up after years of silence

Transformation lives in small, brave steps that shape a new path forward.

Transformation is the willingness to become new. Over and over again.

If you feel like you're unraveling—good. Stay there. Let yourself break open. Let the old version of you dissolve. The cocoon is not a prison. It's a process. On the other side of that process is emergence. Don't fight it.

Who you were is familiar, comfortable, and predictable. But transformation invites you into the unfamiliar, the uncomfortable, the untested. And while that may feel strange for a season, eventually the new ways of thinking, leading, and loving will

become your new rhythm.
And once they do, you'll be ready to rise into the next iteration of
who you were meant to be.

Don't settle for any version of yourself that you've already lived.
Aim for the one you were always destined to become.

That's growth.
That's transformation.
That's leadership with wings.

When you live out the Butterfly Affect Framework—Acceptance,
Growth, and Transformation, something deeper shifts. Not just your
habits or your decisions, but your *affect*—your presence, your
atmosphere, the emotional air you carry into every room. People
may not always have the language for it, but they feel it. They feel
honesty, the steadiness, the openness you've worked hard to build.
And that quiet transformation often becomes one of your greatest
forms of leadership. Long after your words fade, your affect remains
your legacy.

I challenge you:
Tap into what fuels you.
Pay attention to what sparks your energy.
Let your failures become your teachers.
Keep stretching. Keep searching. Keep rising.

Because transformation isn't a moment, it's a mindset.
A daily choice. A way of life.

REFLECTION EXERCISES

1. What moments from your past showed you what truly drives you?

2. Think of a time you failed. What did it teach you about yourself?

3. What activities make you lose track of time because you enjoy them so much?

4. Who are the people in your life who challenge you to grow? How can you spend more time with them?

5. What is one small step you could take this week to stretch beyond your comfort zone?

6. How can you help someone else transform or grow?

7. What old beliefs or habits might you need to release to transform?

Take time to journal your thoughts. Transformation begins with self-awareness.

REFLECTION EXERCISES

Peron 1:

Write the names of two people you would like to help and how.

Person 2:

APPENDIX: TOOLS FOR TRANSFORMATION

This appendix is your **practice space**.

The Butterfly Affect Framework isn't just an idea, it's a way of living. These tools are designed to help you move from insight to action, from inspiration to implementation. Use them at your own pace. Revisit them whenever you feel stuck, stretched, or ready for your next level.

- **Journaling** helps you hear yourself think.
- **Stretch actions** help you grow your leadership in real time.
- **Opportunity reflections** help you say yes to what's in front of you.
- **Whole-self practices** keep your body, mind, and spirit nourished.
- **Celebration rituals** help you honor your progress instead of rushing past it.

Take what you need in this season. Come back for more when you're ready.

Section 1 – Journaling: Your Mirror and Your Map

Journaling is not about buying the perfect notebook and letting it collect dust. It's a verb. It's the raw, honest act of getting thoughts out of your head and onto paper.

Journaling is both **mirror** and **map**:

- A **mirror** that reflects what's really going on inside you.
- A **map** that helps you see where you're heading—and where you want to go.

Why Journal?

Because:

- Your memory is short.
- Your thoughts can lie to you.
- Clarity often shows up on the page before it shows up in your life.

Journaling can help you:

- Notice patterns in your thinking and behavior
- Identify triggers and emotional reactions
- Capture dreams and ideas before they fade
- Track progress on goals and growth
- Find relief when life feels heavy
- Keep your **vision** in front of you daily

How to Start (Simple Format)

You don't need pages of wisdom. You just need consistency—even **three sentences a day** can change your life.

Try this daily format:

1. **What happened today?**
2. **How did it make me feel?**

3. **What do I want to remember or do differently?**

Examples:

"I'm exhausted. I felt invisible in the meeting. But I'm still here. That counts."
"I'm proud of how I handled that difficult conversation. I stayed calm and clear."

Prompts to Get You Going

- What am I grateful for today?
- What's worrying me right now?
- What's one thing I'm proud of?
- What do I want my life to look like a year from now?
- What's one small step I can take today?

Different Styles of Journaling

- **Bullet journaling** – quick lists, tasks, feelings
- **Freewriting** – write without editing or worrying how it sounds
- **Vision journaling** – describe your future life in vivid detail
- **Prayer journaling** – write your conversations with God
- **Art journaling** – doodles, color, and symbols for feelings you can't yet name

Three Keys to Powerful Journaling

1. **Keep it visible**
   Don't hide your journal in a drawer. Keep it where you'll see it—on your nightstand, desk, or in your bag. Flip back often. Let your own words remind you how far you've come.
2. **Keep it repetitive**
   If you're trying to shift habits or grow as a leader, repetition matters. Writing the same goal, scripture, affirmation, or

intention again and again helps rewire your thinking and sharpen your focus.

3. **Link it to visible reminders**
   Pull key phrases, scriptures, or goals from your journal and write them on sticky notes, whiteboards, mirrors, or phone backgrounds. Let your inner work become outwardly visible.

If you can **see it on paper**, you can start building it in your life.

Section 2 – Stretching Your Leadership: 10 "First-Time" Actions

Trying new things opens new doors. Even if you're a seasoned leader, there's always room to stretch.

Choose **one** of these actions to try in the next 24–48 hours:

10 "First-Time" Actions for Seasoned Leaders

1. **Call someone just to thank them—no agenda.**
   Say, "I'm not calling for a favor or a project. I just wanted you to know how much I appreciate what you bring to the team."
2. **Sit silently in a meeting—on purpose.**
   Don't speak unless asked. Observe dynamics, body language, and who steps up when you step back.
3. **Ask a direct report:**
   "What's one thing I do that makes your job more challenging?"
   Listen without defending. Write down what you hear.
4. **Share one personal failure in a team meeting.**
   Tell the story, then connect it to a leadership lesson. Let people see your humanity.
5. **Block two hours of "thinking time" on your calendar—and protect it.**

No meetings, no email, no multitasking. Just thinking, praying, planning, or dreaming.

6. **Let someone else make the final decision.**
   On something you'd normally own, say: "I trust your judgment. I'll support what you choose."
7. **Admit you're stretched.**
   Tell your team, "I'm feeling stretched thin this week. I'm going to lean on you more." Watch how they respond.
8. **Learn one thing about each person's life outside work.**
   Ask, "What's something you're passionate about outside of work?"
9. **Cancel a meeting that no longer serves a purpose.**
   Free that hour for focused work or rest. Tell your team why you're doing it.
10. **Hand the spotlight to someone else.**
    Have a junior teammate lead the next presentation. Introduce them, then sit back and let them shine.

These "firsts" will stretch your humility, curiosity, and courage—the very muscles you need in the Growth and Transformation phases.

Section 3 – Reflection: Saying Yes to Opportunity

Opportunity is generous. It doesn't just knock once. But to recognize it, you must stay **open**, **curious**, and **brave**.

Use this reflection after reading Chapter 11 (Opportunity) or anytime you sense a new door in front of you.

Say Yes – A Short Reflection Practice

Read slowly, then journal your own answers.

Opportunity in real life looks like:

- You say yes to the meeting.
- You speak up in the room.
- You volunteer for the project.
- You start the side venture.
- You introduce yourself.

These small moments become pivot points—the stories you tell later when someone asks, *"How did you get here?"*

Ask yourself:

- **What have I been too afraid to try?**

- **Where have I been waiting for clarity instead of creating it?**

- **What opportunity might be hiding inside a problem I'm currently facing?**

- **If I said "yes" to one brave thing this month, what would it be?**

Opportunity doesn't depend on external validation.
It waits for your **internal decision**.

Section 4 – Feed Your Whole Self (Body, Mind, Spirit)

You cannot lead from emptiness. You weren't designed to.

Leadership requires **energy, clarity, and grounding**, and that means tending to your **body**, **mind**, and **spirit**—not perfectly, but intentionally.

Feed Your Body

- Hydrate throughout the day
- Eat regular, balanced meals
- Move daily (walk, stretch, dance, gentle exercise)
- Honor your body's signals of stress and fatigue

Body Reflection:
Over the next week, one way I will care for my body is:

Feed Your Mind

- Read things that stretch your thinking
- Engage in conversations that challenge your assumptions
- Set boundaries around social media and news
- Seek learning, not just information

Mind Reflection:
One way I will feed my mind this week is:

Feed Your Spirit

- Pray, worship, or meditate regularly
- Spend time with people who lift your faith and hope
- Limit chronically negative voices and environments
- Make space for quiet, gratitude, and reflection

Spirit Reflection:
One way I will nourish my spirit this week is:

A Simple Meditation to Recenter

Try this when you feel overwhelmed:

- Inhale for a slow count of **4**
- Hold for **4**
- Exhale for **4**
- Repeat for 2–5 minutes

This one small practice supports your **body, mind, and spirit** at once.

Section 5 – Celebrate Your Progress

By the time you reach the end of this book, you've done real work—emotionally, mentally, spiritually. Don't rush past that.

Celebration is not fluff. It's fuel.

It:

- Locks in the memory of success
- Builds confidence and courage
- Deepens gratitude and joy
- Strengthens relationships and culture

Quick Reflection: What Needs Celebrating?

Look back over the last 30 days.

- **What is one thing—big or small—that deserves celebrating?**

- **How will I choose to celebrate it?**
  (Rest, ritual, a small gift, a call to my circle, journaling, prayer of thanks, etc.)

Simple Ways to Celebrate

Pick one:

- Write yourself a **victory letter** to read on hard days
- Tell your inner circle and let them cheer with you
- Create a small personal ritual (song, candle, walk, meal)
- Take a photo or video to mark the moment

- Take a real rest day
- Pay it forward—mentor someone, share your story, give to a cause
- Buy something symbolic that reminds you, *"I did that"*

Don't wait only for the huge milestones. Celebrate:

- The day you spoke up
- The boundary you held
- The moment you chose courage over comfort
- The first step toward a new dream

Those inches become the miles.

Final Encouragement

As you move through Acceptance, Growth, and Transformation, remember:

- **Journaling** helps you tell the truth—first to yourself.
- **Stretch actions** help you practice new ways of leading.
- **Opportunity reflections** help you say yes when it counts.
- **Whole-self care** keeps you from burning out while you rise.
- **Celebration** reminds you that your progress is real and worth honoring.

Section 6: Affect Check – A Quick Leadership Reflection

Your affect is the atmosphere you create, your emotional temperature, your presence, the energy people feel when they interact with you. Use this quick check to stay aware and aligned:

Affect Check Questions

1. **What energy did I bring into my spaces today—open or tense?**
   Did people breathe easier around me, or did they tighten?
2. **How might my presence have impacted my team, my family, or the people I encountered?**
   Did I soften a room or harden it? Did I listen, rush, or shut down?
3. **Where did I respond from fear, habit, or pressure—and where did I respond from growth?**
   What patterns am I noticing?
4. **What is one small shift I can make tomorrow to bring a calmer, kinder, more grounded affect?**
   Tone, pace, listening, or simply pausing to breathe.
5. **How do I want people to feel after interacting with me?**
   Seen? Heard? Valued? Safe? Inspired?

Your affect is one of your quietest but most powerful leadership tools. Check it often!

Come back to this appendix often. Write in it. Mark it up. Use it as your **companion** as you develop your own Butterfly Affect—and your own **leadership with wings**.

ACKNOWLEDGEMENTS

This book was shaped by seasons of growth, challenge, and becoming, and I am deeply grateful to those who made this journey possible. I thank God for constant guidance, strength, and purpose, especially in moments of uncertainty. Faith has been my anchor and compass.

To my children, thank you for your love, sacrifices, and unwavering belief. You are my foundation and my greatest source of strength.

To the mentors, leaders, and colleagues who challenged me, supported me, and believed in my potential, thank you for investing in my growth and holding me to a higher standard. Leadership is never a solo journey, and I am grateful for those who walk alongside me.

And to the child I once was, who endured the **Chrysalis** long before she had words for it, thank you for holding on so I could emerge!

Please take a moment to leave a review to help others discover this book. Thank you for your support.